Continue to be u GRITS inspiration!

[signature] 6/26/19

Give Me
G.R.I.T.S.

Girls Raised Intentionally To Succeed

*An ounce of mother
is worth a pound of clergy.*
~Spanish Proverb

Give Me G.R.I.T.S.

Girls Raised Intentionally To Succeed

Terri L. Quinton

Dallas, Texas
www.GiveMeGrits.com

Give Me G.R.I.T.S .
Girls Raised Intentionally to Succeed
Copyright © 2019 Chocolate Diamond Publishing

For information, please contact
Sylvia Dunnavant Hines or Terri Quinton
P.O. Box 2344, Addison TX 75001
Email: info@givemegrits.com
www.givemegrits.com

To contact the author
Email books@terriquinton.com
P: 972.851.5499
www.terri.quinton.com

Printed in the United States of America

Library of Congress Catalog Card Number

IBSN: 978-0-9989574-3-2 (print)
IBSN: 978-0-9989574-2-5 (ebook)

Cover Art: Viola Delgado
Editorial Consultants: Elva Perez and Sandra Clay
Publishing Consultant: Sylvia Dunnavant Hines

Many Thanks To...

I want to thank all the wonderful, strong, creative, passionate women I have had a chance to interview for this project. I also thank each of the mothers who raised us and made us the women we are today. For "when you teach a woman...a family, a community, a nation learns."

May God continue to bless and keep women – and the mothers who raised us.

CONTENTS

She must be something special.
She is. Celebrate her.

--Kobi Yamada

The author's mother, Doris Marie Holt Henderson Lovejoy, next to the home they built in Topeka, Kansas. She is standing next to a tree grown from a sprig the author brought home from grade school.

PROLOGUE

Doris Marie…

When no one cared…you cared
When no one listened…you listened
When no one believed…you believed
When no one cheered…you cheered

When I needed to be taught…you taught
When I needed to be hugged…you hugged
When I needed my space…you surrendered it
When I needed to run instead of walk…you encouraged me
to fly.

More than my "she-ro"…you are in me
You are alongside of me
You are why me
And each day I thank God, who gave me you

One morning as you lazily enter the bathroom you take a rare glance at yourself in the mirror. You halt abruptly. Adjust the glasses you can't see without. Lean in closer to the mirror and inhale a deep breath. For just that single moment, you see it. Maybe it's the intense softness of chocolate brown eyes shadowed by layers of thin fluffy skin, or the fine grooves etched like artist's strokes across your forehead. The silver sprouts of hair rimming your face announce the lineage connection plus the years you've been on this earth. Even the determined jaw set to attack the day and whatever it brings heralds the fused parentage. It is her as surely as if she were standing there saying, "Here we go again!" It's your mother!

Thus began my journey to write this book. I am my mother's daughter. For good or for bad, there is no escaping the imprint! Despite all my protestations when younger, she has left her mark. At twenty, who would ever admit it? At forty, you begin to spot the signs. By fifty, you concede it's real. Your mom is alive in you. The legacy lives on....

This book has been a joyful journey entrusted to me by some amazing daughters and their remarkable mothers. I could not escape my destiny to bring it to life. Like the musician caught up in the tunes playing in their head, this book has shouted "Let me out! Craft my thoughts on paper." The voices and stories would not be ignored. The drumbeat became even louder as a niece and her four little munchkins moved to Dallas, Texas. Watching this young woman struggle, grow and find her way as mother, wage-earner, student and child herself, gave me more reasons to speak these journeys into written existence. This is the book within me, and the legacy honed by remarkable women.

I believe there is a community of women and mothers who are just like me. It has nothing to do with ethnicity or income. It has everything to do with being a woman, mother, sister, niece, female...

My mother was an important part of life. She was my unabashed cheerleader. My guide into adulthood. My listening ear when life threw rotten tomatoes at my dreams. She believed in me like no one else could or has since. For that, I am truly grateful and blessed. I have learned, through my family, through my friends and those whom I have had the fortune to mentor, that this relationship I have had is not always so special for others.

I view the news and movies that portray my ethnic heritage in such a negative light. It appalls me. We are so quick to want to label people and their experiences because it makes us feel comfortable or set above and important. It is a sad way to examine the world and the use of the unique gifts the Creator has bestowed upon each of us.

I did not grow up in a ghetto. I was not introduced to drugs or gangs or abject poverty. Some were and still are. However, these negative scenarios do not define who we are, what we chose to do with our lives.

I lived a charmed (monetarily poor) life growing up. I was loved and wanted. My two parents worked extremely hard to provide the very best they could for my brothers and me. I was expected to succeed. I was expected to go to college (though my parents never had that opportunity). I was expected to do the right thing and help others. Excuses for failing were not part of my upbringing. I know this was true for my friends, as well. More importantly, I believe this view is truer in this great country for many children of color. So, you are black – so what. So, you are a woman – so what. So, your parents were not rich – so what. Forget the media. Cheer the faces of color and the women you see in the films. Root for the athletes with amazing physical prowess who look like you. Read the great scholars of color, the noted women authors and the prescient inventors who made great contributions to our world. This is our true heritage. As Maya Angelou so poignantly wrote, "I rise…!"

We can be more than our circumstances. I learned this from an amazing mother. And so, I began my journey to find the parallel lives in other women in my own circle of support. From the entrepreneurs, business executives, spiritual leaders, home-schooling mothers and more, I was delighted to uncover traces of how much we all are our mother's daughters. I sought to confirm that the foundations we stand on, the journeys we choose, the successes we achieve were erected from the lessons learned from the women who raised us. We are women populated by more reasons we are alike than the divided portrayals spotlighted on television, in the news and at the movies.

This book highlights the "gritty" lessons that have passed from one generation of women to the next – sometimes imperceptibly. They go beyond the simple mom proverbs like "always wear clean underwear because you might get in an accident."

Give Me G.R.I.T.S. – Girls Raised Intentionally to Succeed seeks to capture the essence of womanhood and motherhood in seemingly simple women going about their daily lives. It provides a glimpse into the underpinning lessons of life, faith, family, purpose, health, fun and happiness. These mothers sacrificed so much of themselves to construct the foundation we stand upon today. Hopefully, the lessons shared here can help your passage through life or at least remind you of the important impact other women have played in your journey. And if nothing else, I hope you stop to say THANK YOU to the women who helped shape you into what you are today. Please enjoy the peek into the lives of my remarkable women friends, my BFFs. They have allowed me to connect with them in my life, and I am thankful for a chance to learn more about the extraordinary women who raised them!

He didn't realize that love as powerful as your mother's for you leaves its own mark.
— J.K. Rowling, Harry Potter and the Sorcerer's Stone

PART 1-
Family...Soulful
Shrimp and Grits

Family is not an important thing. It's everything.

--*Michael J. Fox*

*F*amily...*it is the sustaining substance that helped define these* **Girls Raised Intentionally To Succeed***. It's spicy and gritty like* **Soulful Shrimp and Grits.** *Family is challenging. You didn't pick them – but they picked you. Family is genetics and environment all rolled up into one huge element that lends itself to the name we are given, the tools we start out with and the direction we choose to go. Whether dysfunctional, traditional or non-traditional, it is still family. Family is a common factor of these women who found support and direction based upon the family experience. Their values and views of the world and their businesses were crafted by some very strong mothers who set an example for "family first" thinking. The results provided support, confidence and values that defined who they are and how they see the world. As George Santayana, author of "The Life of Reason" explained, "The family is one of nature's masterpieces."*

*The author's mother – Doris Marie Lovejoy (second from the right)
– with many of her childhood friends and co-workers
at her 45th Wedding Anniversary Celebration.
Doris often lunched with these and other ladies.*

ALL GOD'S CHILDREN...

The beauty of the world lies in the diversity of its people.
--Unknown

In 1985 Martha Holcombe Root created a line of black figurines called "All God's Children." Much of her inspiration came from her childhood memories of summers with her brother Tommy on her grandmother's farm. It was a time of simple things like going barefoot, riding the old mule and swimming in the creek. Those figurines touched something in my mom's heart, and she became an avid collector. I am sure they reminded her of her own childhood spent growing up on a small plot of land nestled in North Topeka.

That small-town country living would define her lifelong values and be passed along to her children. My grandmother, Essie Wilson Holt, was the youngest daughter from a family of nine children. Her widowed father would make his way across Louisiana and Oklahoma to eventually call Topeka, Kansas home. They were a close-knit farming people – tilling small plots of land, storing and canning vegetables, raising chickens and celebrating each new addition to the extended family. The men worked other people's orchards and farms. Some like my Grandpa found work with the Santa Fe Railroad. The women ironed and cleaned house for folks in town. Both black and white inhabited the area and displayed truly neighborly values. Help when help was needed. Laughter and conversation when met on the road or working their plots of land.

My mother was born into this reassuring, closed environment, the first child of Essie and Richard Holt. She and her two younger brothers were surrounded by an all-encompassing network of aunts, uncles, cousins and their Grandpa. My mom had two cousins who were only months apart in age from her. Where you saw Doris, you always saw Arlene and Deola. People thought they were sisters, not cousins. Arlene lived around the bend just a couple of miles away. Deola lived in town. Everything centered around the family – cooking, eating, gossiping, holiday celebrations, summer-time firecrackers and wiener roasts, men tossing horseshoes by the creek and children running and laughing in the bright clean sunlight of Kansas.

Schooling was not much different. Long before "Brown vs. the Board of Education" would be fought bringing integration to the city schools, my mom and her brothers would attend country schools composed mostly of white children. It was the country and it was Kansas. Neighbors were neighbors and children were children...then.

Mom would meet and connect in kindergarten with one of her closest and lifelong friends, Mary Ann, a young white neighbor girl. Doris and Mary Ann would continue their friendship even when grown and married. When Mary Ann left for California, the pair exchanged letters and cards throughout their adulthood, stopping only upon Doris Marie's death many years later. Even then, Mary Ann sent condolences to the family.

My mom attended and graduated at seventeen from Seaman High School. Her younger brother was chosen as the "King of the Court" because of his prowess on the football field and not the color of his skin. Mom would eventually find the world a little different from her idyllic country home, but it never deterred her love of talking with people. This color-blind, rose-colored exposure would set the tone for how she interacted with the world and create the "curse" her children felt every time they entered a store or drove around town with her. Mom never met a stranger. If you went shopping with her, you were bound to run into someone she wanted to stop and talk with. Twenty to thirty minutes later, you might make it out of the store and back to the car. She could and would talk to anyone – rich or poor, black or white, thin or fat, short or tall. If they looked her way or even if they didn't, she could find a way to start up a conversation. And...she either knew or was related to more than half of Topeka, or so it seemed. She could light up a room with her conversation and her smile. She had close friends of all cultures and heritage – black, white, Mexican... Later in life, she met regularly with her high school friends (all white) for luncheons, where they gossiped about their children, remembered the old days and talked about who had passed on. That farm-country mentality and the love and closeness of people became a strong lesson for each and every one of her children.

To Doris Marie, all people were family. That lesson has been a cornerstone in my life. My friends marvel at how people will just talk to me – on the street, on a plane, during a networking session. They come from all walks of life and all ethnicities. I tell them it is probably because I make eye contact with people. I seem to be able to walk easily between the white, brown and black world. I have black, white, Latino, Native American and Asian friends. I enjoy the differences, the cultures, the food and the conversations. The unique ambiance each person brings to this world is something only they can bring. I feel a bit sorry for those that look at life with blinders only interacting with "their kind." For me, the lesson taught by my mother is like sampling an amazing dish just cooked for me by my Creator *– a unique version of soulful shrimp and grits!*

Adoptive mother Doris Marie Stokes and daughter Eve Clark

TWO DIFFERENT TYPES OF LOVE

Once there were two women
who never knew each other
One you do not remember,
the other you call Mother.
Which of these two women,
are you the product of?
Both, my darling,
Both, just two different types of love.
--*from the poem Legacy of An Adopted Child, author Unknown*

Not everyone is blessed with two mothers – one who birthed you and one who raised you. Not everyone is fortunate enough as an adult to have a chance to know both mothers and build lasting relationships either. Eve Clark, however, is one of those privileged angels. She is delighted to garner lessons from two mothers. Each plays an important part in her life and provides her the joy of an extended family.

Eve's photogenic smile and easy disposition immediately puts people at ease. She loves clunky jewelry, shoes and more shoes (though the stilettos are now a clear "no-no") and eyeglasses. Around Eve, there is no need to think you are either shy or introverted. She won't give you much chance to talk anyway. Instead, she will revel in sharing stories about her life – her grandbaby, her business, her travel, her shopping deals, her travel, her food, did we say her travel? You name it and she has something to say about it. I am not sure she has ever met a stranger. In a room full of people, even strangers won't be strangers for long. (In that respect, she reminds me of my own mother!)

Eve is the CEO and President of MEB Construction, LLC, a general contracting company in Dallas, Texas. Her construction career has engaged her in tenant finish outs, construction project management, concrete barricade placement and more. She can read a blueprint and conjure up the cost structure as well as any man in the industry.

She is always full of ideas, believes in connecting people to opportunities and each other and knows how to have some fun after working hard. In one of our relaxing moments, I discovered Eve was adopted and had met and built a relationship with her birth mother. The lessons she has learned from her remarkable mothers include family first, staying the course and making time to serve others. It is those family values that add to her spicy disposition and heartfelt connections.

<u>Family First</u>

Doris Marie Stokes ("Mom" to Eve) adopted Eve when she was just a baby. She was a stay-at-home mom who dedicated her life to her husband and family. She loved to sew, cook and work in her garden. She was also an active member in the church and the PTA.

Eve was nurtured by Doris' care and direction. Eve and her brothers attended an all-white Catholic elementary school. Doris wanted the finest education for her children. She often told them to take pride in everything they do no matter how small the task might be. Like many of the mothers in this book, Doris made sure her daughter was exposed to nice clothes, lady-like manners and the best schooling available.

"She was always a lady and wanted me to be one, as well," recalls Eve. "In all my years, I never can remember a harsh word between her and my father. She taught me that you must have peace in your home and from your partner in life to be sustained and content."

Doris believed in "family first" loyalty. This principle intertwined to create a sound foundation for life. Family was everything. Her commitment to the PTA and her children's activities ensured they knew how important they were to her.

"Family will be there when no one else will," often remarked Doris. "Family you can trust. Everyone is not your friend. They might smile in your face and laugh behind your back." She also believed family helped teach you true loyalty, something you can use when choosing your friends and colleagues.

Family commitment spilt over to community involvement with Doris. She was very active in her church. She believed that "giving time is just as important as giving money." You never knew when you would need to be on the receiving end; therefore, it was important to spread goodwill within the community whenever you could.

Eve learned this lesson well. She has been an active participant and leader in several organizations related to construction, minority-owned businesses and Multiple Sclerosis. She reaches out to help other women and minority-owned business owners who want to be in the construction business. She readily shares her knowledge and experiences to help others succeed. Eve has never met a stranger. If you know her, you will soon have a life filled with no strangers as well.

Reunited -- Lesson Learned

"**M**y birth mother was from an entirely different world than the one I grew up in," recalls Eve. "She located me when I was in my early thirties."

*Birth mother Raymona Turner
and daughter Eve Clark*

Raymona Turner lived an all-to-familiar life. She grew up in an abusive household. She was molested and raped at an early age and became pregnant with Eve at age 14. The baby was taken away and given up for adoption. Raymona remained in the household until she was sixteen. She had three more children and battled drug addiction and mental illness most of her adult life. She was defined as mentally disabled and unable to hold a full-time job.

Raymona, however, did not let her traumatic youth and her circumstances defeat her. Even when Eve had given up ever finding and knowing her birth family, Raymona never did. She found Eve when Eve turned 32.

"Despite her challenging upbringing," boasts Eve, "my birth mother has been resilient and has persevered. She obtained her bachelor's degree. I have learned more from her about 'staying the course' in the past few years than I have in my entire life up until I met her. She was never defeated! No matter what she has faces, she prefers to be a conqueror!"

"In grammar school I wanted to be a nun," pronounces Eve. "No one would believe that today!" Eve also wanted to be a mechanical engineer. Her girlfriends were taking Home Economics and Typing classes. Eve hung up her cheerleading outfit and enrolled in shop class – metal works, auto mechanics, woodworking. The schooling would serve her well in her future endeavors.

Perhaps it *IS* in the genes because Eve also was faced with some tough circumstances in her life. She became a mother at sixteen. She gave up her academic scholarships to stay home and raise her son. She worked numerous jobs as a young mother to provide for herself and her son. She continued her education and eventually became an optician.

"I would say that this life chose me," declares Eve. "I was an optician up until the time I developed Multiple Sclerosis. After spending two years barely walking, I became better." Eve is not 100%, but you would never know it talking to her or seeing her. She decided to manage her illness instead of it managing her. You can find her on the construction site wearing her yellow or pink hard hat, telling a crew what to do and how to do it. She has traveled the world and been the guest of ambassadors, seen amazing countries, met exciting people, enjoyed unique foods and reveled in diverse cultures. Eve has been slowed in gait, but that has not decelerated her movements one bit when it comes to doing the things she likes to do. She's neither defeated nor bowed down!

After being on disability for two years, Eve moved from Chicago (home) to Dallas. She decided to slowly rejoin the workforce. As God would have it, she began working with a friend rehabbing duplex buildings in the evenings just for the sheer sport of it. He taught her how to read blueprints, install toilets, tile floors, hang drywall, install carpet, put in hot water tanks and much more. That led to an actual paying job with a small facility repair firm that did work for national retailers.

After three years of working with the facilities repair company, Eve found the impact upon her health was taking its toll. She couldn't keep up the demanding 24/7 schedule. While working at the firm, Eve met a lady, Becky Whelan, who had three young children at home and a severely ill husband. In 2006, Eve and Becky left the employee world and opened the doors of MEB Construction.

Today, Eve, now sole owner of the firm, boasts being able to drive anything with an engine and shoot a rifle better than most men. All you must do is see her making the rounds at a construction site, and you will become a believer. Though Eve didn't become a mechanical engineer, we would all agree that owning a construction company is a great consolation prize. And, she has never given up despite health issues. Various episodes with MS have at times left her mute and unable to walk. Eve continues to claw back. She has rehabbed her body and returned to the life she wants to live. She's neither been defeated nor bowed down!

Sometimes two is better than one, and Eve certainly has had the opportunity to learn that lesson from her two extraordinary, different and wonderful mothers.

Vicky Teherani

WEALTH IS FAMILY...NOT FORTUNE

The love of family and the admiration of friends is much more important than wealth and privilege.

--Charles Kuralt

Expect laughter. Expect excitement. Expect energy. Her eyes light up as she talks. She is in constant motion, making sure all her guests are enjoying themselves. It seems a little strange coming from a CFO ("number cruncher") turned CEO. But, then, you haven't been around Vicky Teherani. She loves people and people love her. Vicky is short,

Chinese by birth, American by style and smart by heredity. She is also generous with her time, talent and money, focused on her lifelong ambition of uplifting others.

When I first met Vicky, she was the CEO and one of the principals of Rolland Safe and Lock Company. She has since left the position of CEO and spends more time growing with her investment capital company (More 2 Wealth), offering advice to start-up firms and mentoring graduate students.

I met Vicky by happenstance (or through a touch of God's ingenuity). She was invited to attend a Dallas Cowboys game by one of the national banks – no doubt wanting to woo her and her account to their bank. I attended because my business partner could not go, and she knew I loved the Dallas Cowboys. As fate would have it, Vicky's husband became ill and one of her employees and his wife attended instead. A short email to Vicky telling her she missed a great game and that I hoped to meet her one day resulted in us enjoying breakfast together at a quaint little café not far from where we both lived. We found we had several things in common – running a company, a love of sports, a taste for good wine and a willingness to not be defined strictly by our culture.

Since then, our burgeoning friendship has found us sharing time together at events designed to help some cause or other. I laughed when Vicky invited me to attend a Safari Club event in downtown Dallas. Did she not know my distaste for guns and hunting? As it turned out, it became a learning experience for me. I found the Safari Club was more than hunting and shooting. Conservation and saving the environment were key principals of the organization. I also found out Vicky is one of the luckiest people I have ever met. Sitting at her table surrounded by friends and co-workers (all women), we laughed, talked, ate and enjoyed wine and champagne. Vicky bought tickets for the raffle and proceeded to give a ticket to each woman at the table. Several won some magnificent prizes. The grand prize was a fur jacket. Wouldn't you know it, Vicky won the grand prize!! She modeled it for everyone, took pictures wearing it and allowed others to do the same. Her generous nature conceded the jacket to the wife of one of her partners. Unbelievable! However, it turns out Vicky had won the grand prize the year before from the tickets she bought for her guests. She had already won a jacket the year before and saw no need for two. See what I mean about her luck!

Vicky credits both her parents for who she is today; but she loves and admires her mom for so many lessons learned…including family, tenacity, humility and an adventuresome spirit.

<u>Wealth Deferred</u>

Bow In Chan was born in China. Her grandfather was a scholar. In the olden days, scholars were given land and money and were supported for life by the government. His children and grandchildren flourished from his honored position. Bow In Chan was well educated, her family was wealthy and like her grandfather and parents, she never worked outside the home.

However, she met a young man whose mother had died when he was only nine. He was from a very poor family, but he was gentle, kind and industrious. Bow left the life of privilege to marry and work with him.

Vicky Teherani and her mom,
Bow In Chan

"My mother never worked a day in her life until she married my dad," recalls Vicky. "Together they were small business owners and raised all eight of us children. She never complained about leaving her life of wealth for her family. Instead, she put everything she had into the family."

t to the market daily to buy groceries and prepared three meals a day for the family of ten. She washed clothes and helped her children with homework.

"Her love is unconditional," says Vicky. "If she has two apples, she will give you the larger one. If she only has one, she will give it to you."

Bow at the writing of this book, was in her mid-nineties. She had lived with Vicky and her family for many years and

27

several years ago returned to Hong Kong to be with her other children and family members. While in the states, Bow was actively engaged helping to raise her grandchildren. She enjoyed cooking meals for the family daily. She washed clothes, remembered all the birthdays, including grandchildren and spouses, and still found time to gamble and have fun. She enjoyed sharing a meal with anyone who came her way. "She loves my husband as her own son," states Vicky. "She is happiest when she is helping and serving others (literally serving some great food). In high school, I invited some friends home for lunch almost daily. My mom served us with a smile. As I grew older, I understood the sacrifice on her part. She had to determine how to divide a fish meant for ten people to make sure it could serve two extra visitors to the house. "

Vicky has the same generous nature. Besides giving away the fur coat, she readily shares advice, connections to organizations and more. She has a daughter and a son and like any mother is concerned about them and their choices. You can see the love as she discusses their life choices and direction. She is proud that they, too, understand it is about family, friends and relationships above wealth and power.

Reach for the Top

"**M**y mother owned a tool shop," recalls Vicky. "She was so smart that if she saw a tool in high demand, she would buy up the production from the factory, so other companies would have to come to her to buy it. She knew how to leverage her buying power."

Vicky learned her negotiation skills from watching her mom in the tool shop. Bow would negotiate with suppliers on price and quantity discounts while keeping an ever-watchful eye on the marketplace and opportunities.

Bow focused on getting everything done and sought to inspire her children to be the best they could become. She never complained when she had to work hard to help the family survive and thrive.

Bow also never gave up in achieving her dreams. She came to the U.S. at age 65. She has always been prepared to take up a challenge and not knowing English was a challenge for her. She used to tell Vicky, "It is always the first time for anyone. But when you do it the second time for the same task, you must be better than others." Bow took that to heart as she sought to pass the citizenship test and become a U.S. citizen. She wanted to be able to vote and, thus, she had to be a citizen. After failing the English portion of the test twice, she passed it the third time (by then she was 80, and they allowed her to have a translator in the meeting.) It took her 10 years to achieve her goal of citizenship, but she did it. When she went to get her passport photo, the administrator told her not to smile. Bow was having none of that! She had one of the widest and most defined smiles ever seen on a U.S. passport photo. Never give up! "I believe my drive to be the best," remarks Vicky, "comes from my mom. I can't say I grew up with a specific ambition. I was raised to 'go all the way.' There is no limit to one's ability – the only limit is in our head. She also encouraged me to not be afraid to try anything. No matter where I worked or what the job was, I always wanted to get to the top job."

Vicky learned this lesson well. She arrived in the U.S. set to go to the university and study social work. She wanted to help others. However, she soon discovered her English wasn't good enough to understand the psychology classes. A classmate told her to try accounting; she was good in math.

Accounting paid off for Vicky. She worked for Belo Corporation for more than fourteen years, where she started as a treasury analyst and rose to be the first woman officer as their Vice President-Treasurer and then Vice President – Controller and General Manager of Management Services.

Once she reached the top of the financial side, Vicky decided she wanted to be CEO of a company. To do that, she knew she had to have some sales and operational experience. She left Belo and went to work for Prime Art and Jewel (PAJ), one of the largest silver wholesalers in the world. She became the Chief Operating Officer at PAJ. Then, she became the general manager of Brands88, the branded jewelry company that held several licenses including the Elle brand.

From there, Vicky formed a venture capital company and ended up investing and working with one of her PAJ vendors – Rolland Safe & Lock Company. Rick Rolland convinced her to come to work for them as one of the owners. She did and eventually moved into the top spot.

"It is easier to help others when you are the decision maker and not just the follower," states Vicky.

Like Bow, Vicky learned to persevere and be committed. It has helped drive her to secure her dream at the top. Now, she spends time helping others and her children achieve financial security and their dreams.

Okay ... I Don't Know

"**M**y mom had four boys before she had me, her first girl," recalls Vicky. "She knew nothing about how to handle a little girl – how they should dress, how they should be. My aunt (my mom's youngest sister) shopped for me and took me under her wings to make sure I dressed appropriately for my gender."

Vicky recalls that Bow was not threatened by the closeness between Vicky and her aunt. Bow displayed no ego. She only thought about what was best for her daughter. She focused only on Vicky's academic achievements. If Vicky made good grades, Vicky could do anything she wanted. As an example, though her mom was conservative, Vicky wore the shortest skirts in high school and her mom never said a word.

Bow also taught Vicky to respect everyone. You can see it in how she deals with the various workers and American culture. Bow would tell Vicky, "Sometimes the smartest person in the room may be the quietest person in the room. You don't have to show others how smart you are. You just need to continue to use your smartness to serve others."

Life is an Adventure

Bow has always enjoyed trying out new things. She taught herself how to garden in the Texas soil and weather. She made clothes for her grandchildren. She still exercises every day to stay healthy and does not complain about anything.

She has always enjoyed meeting new people. Bow feels that one can appreciate every walk of life and learn from the differences. The differences are the best part of knowing and learning about other people. The more different we are, the better and stronger we all become. After all, Bow says, "If we are all the same, we only need one human being in the world."

Vicky believes in Bow's philosophy of life. It's why she is so outgoing and tolerant of others. It only takes a short conversation to realize she is much like her mother in this regard.

When Bow lived in the states with Vicky and her family, she traveled between Hong Kong and the United States. The family used to have someone travel with her to make sure she made all the airport connections. However, Bow told the family that she could do it on her own if they got her to the gate. That independent nature is what keeps Bow young and ever learning. It is also why Vicky is so independent and relies on herself first in trying to handle a situation before reaching out to others.

Bow still lives her life to the fullest back in Hong Kong. She drinks, plays mahjong and loves being around her family. Nothing bothers her, and she thinks life is the biggest playground. She has a kid's heart and reminds her family to stay young in mind and heart. Bow, I think you have taught Vicky well! She certainly believes in keeping her mind active, having fun, serving others and living life to its fullest!

Author's family photo celebrating parents' 45th wedding anniversary – Front Row, seated – Doris Marie Lovejoy and Lawrence Lovejoy (mom and dad). Back Row from left to right – Lawrence Darryl Lovejoy, Larry Henderson, author Terri L Henderson Quinton, Lance Lovejoy and Kevin Lovejoy

LOVE, NOT BLOOD…

You must be a special lady
And a very exciting girl
You gotta be a special lady
'Cause you got me
sitting' on top of the world
Oh, sittin' on top of the world
--Harry Ray, Al Goodman and L. Walter

Normal (whatever that is)… Dysfunctional (aren't we all)… Blended (buzzword for today)…. No matter how far we roam or what we do in life, family has an impact upon our lives.

I don't know when I realized my family was a little different. I had a mom and a dad. I had a big brother and little brothers. I was the only girl and was encompassed by love and laughter from an extended family of grandparents, aunts, uncles and cousins who called Topeka, Kansas home. We seemed like every other family in our neighborhood – black, working-class parents, poor or lower middle class, a mom and a dad who toiled long hours to make a better life for our family. For me, it was a charmed life. My older brother and I were the first grandchildren of my mother's parents and they loved and showered us with so much love and attention – more than anyone could even imagine. We didn't know what we didn't have, but, more importantly, we didn't care. What we did have was plenty of love. We spent lots of time at my grandparents' home in the country, while mom and dad worked overtime to save money to build a house for our family.

When I was four, I started kindergarten in one of Topeka's segregated city schools because that is where my babysitter lived. (My older brother attended the country school for his first few years of schooling.) My mom had a little baby girl a few months after I started school. Lavera died just three months after her birth. (I don't know how my Mom coped with the death. She was only 26 when it happened). And so, instead of me having a little sister, I remained the baby of our family for another four years.

When I was eight, my mom gave birth to a beautiful baby boy – my very own little brother! He had a different name than mine, and I realized there was something a little different about our family.

My mom explained that I was a Henderson. My "real" father loved my brother and me so much that he implored my mom never to change our names after the two of them divorced shortly after my birth. He had taken pride in naming both of us. He carried around a baby book while my mom was pregnant, and he chose Larry Dean (my big brother) and Terri Lee (me) as our names. My mother agreed.

When my mom met and married my dad (the man who loved and raised me), each of their children (my little brothers) carried my dad's name, Lovejoy. It was a little confusing in my early years, but to my mom it was just the way life was. It didn't matter about the name. We're all one family.

She taught me early that family was more than birthing a child. It was about loving, nurturing and raising a child. Mom loved ALL her children equally, but because each of us was unique, her love stretched to encompass our uniqueness. Some of us needed more attention, while others blossomed with just a smile and pat. She encouraged us, scolded us and pampered us like no one in our lives ever would. My brothers learned to cook, sew and type (she did not want them entering the military carrying guns if they could sit in the office and type).

While others considered the man who raised me as my stepfather, and my younger brothers as my stepbrothers or half-brothers, my mom made sure those words did not exist in our home. We were a whole family – nothing half or step about us! We were all her children – brothers and sisters – regardless of our names. My brothers were not half anything – they were all whole. We lived, loved, played, celebrated and grew up together as one family. Mom taught us "it is not where the blood comes from, but where the love comes from" that makes a family. Even today, my brothers and I are all very close. It is the gift that keeps on giving with nieces, nephews, grandnieces, and grandnephews. We each knew the power of a mother's love and set out to conquer our world based upon her example.

By the way, that love of people and family extended to my biological father, as well. Despite my mom's differences with my father in her early life (two very young headstrong individuals), she never said a disparaging word about him. She encouraged us to visit him – though I really didn't see the point until I was much older. My mom wanted us to know who he was. She and he were friendly until her death. Eventually, I, too, built a relationship with him. Her persistence in me knowing him gave me another family and a further understanding of my heritage much later in my life after she and my dad who raised me, passed away. My biological father became ill and was unable to drive. I brought him to Texas to live with me. He was in his eighties at the time, and we had a passing relationship until this experience. I will always believe God and my mother had a conversation and said, these two need to know each other better. They are family!

My father and I built a wonderful relationship before he passed away. He lived with me for two years, and I learned so much about him, my mom, their love, his love for my brother and me and his side of the family. I now have a few cousins I stay in contact with because of him. My love for jazz, photography, gadgets, computers, peach cobbler, homemade chili, and so much more all coincided with his love for the same things. And… I know so much more about my gene pool and the power of love between family members. (But this is all for another book and another time.)

PART 2 - True Grit(s)

Woven together by love.
Strengthened together by love.
--*Unknown*

It wasn't the cowboys who had **TRUE GRIT**. *It was the women behind them and the women in this book. Some people are handed fortune and fame on a silver platter with a silver spoon. They may be viewed as the fortunate in life. However, it is the struggles, setbacks and mountains that define the dash between birth and death. That dash, that journey, is richer and more meaningful and the achievements more appreciated when it takes* **TRUE GRIT** *to get there. The mothers in this book didn't necessarily talk about their struggles. They viewed them as a part of life. And the success of their lives was dependent upon overcoming those struggles and passing a lesson along to their daughters that they, too, could overcome. We've all heard the truism "You never fail until you stop trying."(Albert Einstein) These mothers showed the way and we are eternally grateful for their examples!*

Bonnie Nijst with her mom,
Jeanette Hermine Chompff Nijst (Jane)

IN CHARGE

Mother, the ribbons of your love are woven around my heart.

--Unknown

She is easily recognizable in a room full of people. She is gracious, inquisitive and vivacious. You will find her in an intense conversation, with her full attention targeted on an individual. Whether challenging the norm, selling her ideas or conveying a process designed to lead to a solution, she is often the one in charge of the dialogue. You can't help but listen, respond and reflect on what she is saying. Shiny onyx hair, twinkling coal eyes and an upturned smile create the image of Bonnie Nijst. What you see is exactly what you get! She is a confident woman. Bonnie is that rare creative person who sells, creates and processes all at the same time.

"When I was a little girl," recalls Bonnie, "I don't remember having a particular career in mind. I just remember wanting to be in charge. At the time, the ultimate for me was to be a vice president. It sounded so prestigious, and I certainly didn't know any women with that title. I thought that was the highest position you could have."

Bonnie now knows there are a few higher levels than vice president. She has found both as the CEO and President of FIDGET Branding, a B2B growth marketing agency specializing in small, medium-sized and diverse businesses and under-resources divisions of large enterprises.

Bonnie is a hard worker, a lesson learned from her mother. She also credits her mother with the role family plays in her life today.

A Legacy of Hard Work

Jeanette Hermine Chompff Nijst (nicknamed Jane) is why this country of mosaic cultures excels. It is another immigrant's story – one of hard work and low pay, producing a family of achievers and contributors to our great nation.

In the early 50's, Indonesia had been freed from the colonial rule of the Dutch. Jane, her husband Jules and their family were part of the Dutch-Indonesians. They were less welcome in their homeland after independence. The family decided to leave their tropical homeland to stake their future in The Netherlands. But the climate there was not friendly to a family used to sun-kissed rays from the equator. Jane's husband and Bonnie's father decided to unite with his brother in America. He left the family behind until he could get settled in Los Angeles. Jane followed her husband in 1960 to a new land and new home.

"My mom arrived in New York with all three of us after having traveled all the way from Holland by boat," says Bonnie. "I was only a year old. My brother and sister were seven and eight. Mom didn't speak a word of English. She found her way to the train station with all three of us in tow and boarded the train to take us clear across America to Los Angeles to reunite with my father. She was just thirty-one years old. I can't imagine the courage it took to do that!"

One of Jane's first objectives was to learn English and she began by enrolling in night school. After that she went to school to study data processing and found a job in downtown Los Angeles. Every day, she would take the bus from the suburbs, where the family lived, to her data processing job. But her hard work didn't end there. In 1967, the family opened a restaurant. In the evenings after Jane and her husband completed their day jobs, they would come home, change clothes, and run the restaurant. They both worked every day of the week – Monday through Friday at their day jobs and Tuesday through Sunday at their restaurant. Jane could be found cutting up chickens, chopping meat until her wrists hurt and then mopping floors at midnight. They did this for twenty years.

Bonnie was introduced to hard work early. When her older brother and sister grew up and moved out, Bonnie became a latch-key child at age eleven. She would come home from school, clean up the house, cook her dinner and stay up late waiting for her parents to come home.

"Dad would often encourage me to stay up and watch Johnny Carson with him," recalls Bonnie. "Sometimes I wouldn't get to bed until one o'clock in the morning! I guess that's why I am still a night owl and can function on five or six hours of sleep."

Bonnie also helped in the restaurant. Her mother would be in the back kitchen, handling food preparation. Bonnie would work in the front kitchen, timing the meals and putting out the actual food orders. She worked alongside her mother for over fifteen years in the restaurant business, only stopping when they closed the restaurant in 1987 when her father suddenly became ill.

Today, Bonnie still works hard in business development. After seventeen years in sales, sales management, public relations, marketing and communications with companies like PR Newswire, Medialink Worldwide, Medialink Corporate Television and Marketwire, she joined her husband's agency, ZEESMAN. Initially, she was the business development person. She bought the majority interest in the firm in 2003 and became its CEO and

President. In 2019, they relaunched and repositioned the agency as FIDGET Branding.

"I have always gravitated to smaller and more entrepreneurial environments," says Bonnie. "I think the autonomy of smaller firms fits my personality best. Besides, my family is full of entrepreneurs. My parents, my sister, my brother, my nephews and my nieces have all been business owners. It was a natural progression for me."

Bonnie's experience in the growth of the agency is built upon hard work and commitment. When a uniform company came to them for a brand assessment and marketing program, they had to tell the company the truth about their existing program before they could proceed any further. During the assessment of the brand, they discovered several internal challenges that had to be addressed before a successful marketing program could be developed. The agency recommended that the uniform company fix the challenges and then return to have a discussion on their brand. Four years later, they returned to have Bonnie's team develop a new corporate identity, an overarching branding platform, a new website and seasonal in-store marketing programs. The results included a doubling of the client's business, as well as numerous industry and client awards.

"Having grown up in the restaurant business with my parents, service has always been meaningful to me then and now," relates Bonnie. "We served our customers then just as we serve our clients' best interests today. Our focus is first and foremost on the relationship – not the transaction."

Bonnie also says her mother helped her career and her focus on business in another way. It was the things she didn't say to her.

"She never told me to get married, be quiet, find a man, settle down or hurry up and have a baby," says Bonnie. "She never told me business wasn't a place for a woman. She didn't understand what I did, but she was always my champion and proud of me. She provided me with an incredible amount of freedom to live life on positive terms with integrity and joy."

Take Care of Family

In 1986, Jane's world turned upside down. Bonnie's father was diagnosed with leukemia. Jane put her family first and made the only decision that mattered. She took a leave of absence from work and took care of

Jane with baby Bonnie

her husband around the clock for a year. She could be found sleeping in the hospital, warming blankets, feeding him and keeping him company.

Ten years later, Bonnie was having a difficult pregnancy. Jane did not hesitate one minute to stay with her daughter when the three-month premature birth of Jules occurred.

"Without a second thought, my mom put her life on hold again and moved in with us," remembers Bonnie. "She fed, bathed and cared for Jules for the first three years of his life. She always said it was the best job she'd ever had … and it was one that only ended when Mom had a stroke. That shifted the balance of the relationship between my son and her. Now, it was my three-year-old holding his 70-year-old grandmother's hand to help her slowly navigate the hospital corridor."

Jane's family-above-all-else lesson resonates with Bonnie. Family is important to her. She works with her husband in their business – a different perspective. She thinks her son Jules is an old soul. His bedroom is decorated with photos of his grandmother and grandfather (whom he never knew) and he tells Bonnie he misses them as if he knew them both.

Bonnie credits her mother with teaching her about work, love, life and her Indonesian culture. They are the lessons that have defined Bonnie's life, shaped her business and created a legacy for Jules.

Sylvia Dunnavant Hines and her adoptive mom
Austria Marie Robinson

NEVER GIVE UP

Not flesh of my flesh, nor bone of my bone, but still miraculously my own. Never forget for a single minute, you didn't grow under my heart but in it.

—*Fleur Conkling Heyliger*

I met Sylvia Dunnavant Hines in a most unusual way. I co-owned a print shop in Dallas, Texas with my husband. We had bought a new large machine to do quality full color printing easier and faster. We decided to market our abilities through a postcard direct mail campaign. About six months after the campaign, this wide-smiling, bright-eyed, fast-talking young lady came into our shop with one of our postcard mailers in her hand. She wanted to talk to someone about printing some flyers and registration forms for an upcoming 5K Run. It was to raise money for breast cancer support of women of color.

It didn't take long for us to realize we had made a real connection. Her non-profit, called Celebrating Life Foundation, was doing amazing work with breast cancer survivors to provide support and assistance. The 5K Run was designed to raise money, bring mammogram testing to those without insurance and help women enjoy a day of healthy fun activities and food. I couldn't resist helping her. My mom had breast cancer and was a survivor. Plus, this young woman (soon to become an ordained minister), was passionate and committed to her cause. I not only enlisted to help with the printing, but also became part of her advisory board for a time.

I found out she had written a book called *"Celebrating Life"* with stories and amazing photos of women who were survivors. She was a journalism major in college and had put her skills to work around subjects she cared about. She was and is an amazing photographer (see my latest headshot on the back cover) and publishes books. Her fervor for her faith, cancer survivors and writing have never wavered. Find out for yourself what makes Sylvia tick.

Contributed by Sylvia Dunnavant Hines

When I was a little girl, having two mothers seemed like having two heads. It was unnatural and made me feel weird. Many times, I kept this dilemma to myself. Most people thought my adopted mother was the only mother I had. However, there were the awkward holidays or special occasions when my birth mother, Jan Walton, came around. Then, I had to explain this woman I resembled so much.

Once I got over my childish fears of someone knowing about my two mothers, I realized that I was very blessed. I was blessed that my birth mother had grasped that she was not capable of raising me. I was extremely fortunate that God had given her the desire to make sure I was placed in very capable hands.

Austria Marie Robinson possessed those very capable hands. Even though I was only four years old when I went to stay with her, I still remember that day. There was something special about her. I knew from the day that I first laid eyes on her that I never wanted to leave her. She was undoubtedly one of the most loving and compassionate women I have ever met.

My mother was a very wise and witty woman. She always had a catchy phrase or word of knowledge about any given situation. When I was growing up, I was always amazed at the stories that she told and the parables she carried in her spirit. Without notice, she would interject a funny story that brightened even the darkest of days.

Yet, the most valuable lesson that I learned from her would come at a time when I thought her teachings were over. I had reached the end of my rope, but nobody knew it. I was 27 years old and I had just given birth to my son, Jaysen. I was a single parent and knew nothing about raising a child. Even though people had told me that everything was going to be okay, I had serious doubts.

After giving birth to a baby boy that was over 9 pounds, my body had been stretched beyond belief. As I was trying to prepare for what was next, my mind was exhausted, my body was fatigued, and I felt overwhelmed.

Then, my mother arrived! She was determined to help take care of her first grandchild. As much as I wanted her there, a part of me was afraid to let her know how terrified I was of being a single mom. There was no way I could share the depth of my concerns with her. (This was more than three decades ago and having a child outside of marriage was not a popular thing to do.) God has always given my mother an intuitive nature that has allowed her to tap into almost any situation in my life. This time would be no exception.

The night before she arrived, I had tried to fry some chicken. I don't know what I did wrong, but it was a mess. I was too weak to take it downstairs and throw it out, so I wrapped it up in some foil and placed it in the refrigerator.

Once my mother had settled in, she asked if I had anything to cook for dinner. I told her about the chicken that I had messed up and that I had a head of cabbage in the vegetable bin. "What do you mean, you messed up the chicken?" she asked, as she washed her hands and headed toward the stove. Before I could explain, she took the chicken out of the refrigerator and started tossing pots and pans around. She grabbed some spices out of my cabinet and began to season the chicken. She chopped up the cabbage and began to mix up some hot water cornbread. The smell coming from the kitchen began to fill my small apartment. In no time at all she was placing plates on the table and notifying me that dinner was ready. There is no other word for it, the food was simply fabulous. I couldn't believe it. I couldn't believe how good it tasted and how wonderful it felt to have her presence there. I went back for a third helping!

When I was at my weakest moment, without saying a word, my mom taught me one of my most valuable lessons. You can never give up. God specializes in using the unusable. I felt like my life was symbolic of the chicken. My mother had added a few spices and a little flour and turned an old dish into a delicacy. I was ready to throw out the chicken and had no idea how to manage my life. But all I needed was God to step in and add a few spices and seasonings.

Whenever I face a storm in my life, I reflect on this moment. No matter what the situation is, I imagine my mother just adding some spices and turning it around. Although my mother was an amazing cook, I know that God is the ultimate chef. It was her quiet spirit and tenacious hold on life that let me realize there wasn't anything that God couldn't handle.

Sylvia Dunnavant Hines and her birth mother Jan Walton

One More Lesson

Less than six months after my adopted mother passed away, my birth mother Jan became very sick. Out of her three children, I was the one who had to be her caregiver. Her illness placed me in a situation of spending more time with her as an adult than I had in my entire life.

All my life Jan had been a very complicated person, so getting to know her wasn't easy. Once she ended up staying with me, I became the brunt of the bitterness she had been dealing with for years. At first, it was very difficult. Then one day, I walked in and overheard her speaking to herself. She was saying some very hateful things to herself. I suddenly realized that she couldn't be any nicer to me than she was to herself.

After several months, we finally found a happy medium to communicate with each other. Then, one day I overheard her talking in the bathroom. She was looking in the mirror and once again she was spewing some very hateful words to herself. I walked in the bathroom, placed my hand on her face and told her how beautiful she was. I reminded her of the many things that she had accomplished in her life. She jokingly looked me in the eyes and responded, "And, you are such a liar!" We both laughed. Then she hugged me and the words that she was saying seemed to disappear into thin air.

There is no doubt that my birth mother had experienced much pain in her life. Yet, I realized after spending prolonged time with her that a soft word can heal the hardest of hearts. Whenever she would get agitated or say something nasty, I would remind her that I loved her.

Amazingly enough, it was the love that I received from my adopted mother that allowed me to love and care for Jan. All my life I wanted to spend time with my biological mother. I never thought that it would come about this way. As my adopted mother would say, "God always has a plan."

Marilyn Pinson (right) with her mother,
Ada Mae Sneed

DEAL MAKER

We don't get a handbook on life; Instead, God blesses us with insightful mothers.

--Marilyn Pinson

Reddish blond curly hair, hazel brown eyes and a ready smile, "The Professor," as she was called by her childhood friends, is smart, witty, spiritual, reflective and respected. Marilyn Pinson is an active professional and supply chain specialist at Nokia of America. She ensures diverse suppliers (women, minorities, veterans and small businesses) have a chance to participate in Nokia purchasing opportunities. "Because I have a servant's heart, God has placed me in a position where I can serve minority and women-owned businesses," notes Marilyn.

Serving others is what Marilyn does. She is active in organizations, assisting women and minority business owners to grow and develop their companies. She participates in establishing educational programs designed to aid them in succeeding in today's economy. Marilyn has been instrumental in insuring existing minority and women suppliers remain in the supply chain despite consolidation, cut-backs and changes within the purchasing processes. She is an award-winning advocate on behalf of minority and women suppliers.

I met Marilyn at the Dallas/Fort Worth Minority Supplier Development Council. We engaged in conversation around business, of course. But we eventually realized both of us liked to write. That began a whole different dialogue. Marilyn participated part-time as a *Dallas Morning News* Community Columnist and had several columns published by the newspaper. She found the joy of writing return to her only to lose it for a while when her grandmother, Mobie, passed away at age ninety-nine. When asked to participate in this book, she naturally put her writing skills back to work to provide some wonderful lessons and colorful stories surrounding her and her mother.

Respect Yourself and Others

Ada Mae Sneed (Cheapie) never attained her high school diploma, but you wouldn't know that by the way she managed her daughters, husband and guests. She became a young mother at seventeen, when Marilyn's older sister Jocelyn was born.

"We grew up calling her Ada," articulates Marilyn. "Some people find it odd and some may consider it disrespectful. However, the only answer I can give them is that they didn't know Ada. She was the type of woman who commanded the room when she entered. In business, there are things called 'deal breakers.' If Ada was not on board, it was a deal breaker."

Ada was also a deal maker! She taught her three daughters to respect her and the adults around her. It was not an option; it was expected. The mention of Ada's name to her daughters would cause them to change their attitude and disposition quickly. She raised her daughters with a firm hand but encouraged them to give people a chance.

Ada lived during a time when African-American women were called "girl" in the South no matter how old they were. Yet, when her girls were integrated into an all-white school, she did not allow her experiences to influence their perception of people.

"She told me a number of times," recalls Marilyn, "that she was just a baby trying to raise babies. I believe where we arrive in life is a conscious choice, and Ada demonstrated that through the way she lived her life. I learned early in life that respect is not earned by what a person calls you; it is how they see you that counts. I appreciate the gift she gave me in respecting all people and giving them a chance."

Perhaps that is one of the reasons Marilyn so easily fits in working with ethnically diverse businesses. She has a healthy respect for others, their cultures, their skills and their challenges. She collaborates internally with her colleagues in locating and utilizing diverse suppliers. That requires her to visit supplier locations, as well as talk with them about improvements in their processes and operations, challenges they face and successes they experience. For Marilyn, it is a work of joy in the setting where God has placed her.

Managing the Deal

A young deal maker, Ada Mae Sneed

Ada's nickname was "Cheapie." Marilyn didn't really know why her mother was called that but drew her own conclusions when she was about 7 or 8 years old.

"I was playing in the background in the presence of a visitor," recollects Marilyn. "I heard the visitor ask Cheapie, 'How'd you get that nickname?' I bellowed out before I could catch myself, 'Because she's cheap!' I knew as soon as our guest left, I would have to pay the piper, but all my mother did was laugh and tell me my quick-witted response or 'capping' I got from my grandfather's people."

Ada was thrifty. The times required it. She was the Chief Financial Officer (CFO) of the family and Chief Executive Officer (CEO) managing the lives in the family. Every other Friday, her husband would come home and lay his paycheck on the TV. Ada would give him an allowance, and the rest of his check would go toward taking care of the family and building a savings. She was the advisor both her husband and her children sought. Her insight and skills helped her husband make sound financial decisions.

"When I was in elementary school, my Dad's union went on strike," remembers Marilyn. "Ada advised him not to join the strike because we were a young family and he was our only source of income. I recall him getting threats. He would sit in the living room holding a shotgun, as we cringed in a back bedroom. Due to his stance, doors opened internally for him after the strike. Management's view of him changed and he was promoted into a supervisory position."

Ada pushed, nudged, and directed other facets of the family life, as well. She pressed her daughters to get the highest education possible. She set standards for them based upon what she believed they could achieve. You did not bring a "C" grade into her house. If you couldn't decide on the direction to go, or you thought the decision was too hard to handle, Ada would make it for you. Indecision was no decision at all. She had a vision for her family that was fully supported by her husband.

Ada's management meant she had to sacrifice a lot herself to make sure her girls had bright futures. She attended all the school activities. And even though her husband could not always be present, she reminded the girls that he was the reason they could do the things they did. Like any great CEO she believed in giving credit where it was due.

"I can't remember a day going hungry or a sense of helplessness when growing up," affirms Marilyn.

Ada's oversight extended to the kitchen, as well. Ada was a great cook. She used to prepare the best holiday dinners.

"She would have us up all night creaming butter and sugar for her baked goods, while we listened to soulful music," says Marilyn. "In our family, Ada was well known for her egg pies and lemon pies. She eyeballed everything – there were no recipes."

Marilyn's dad, "Shorty" used to tell Ada when they got married, "Cook whatever you want, as long as it doesn't kill us!" When Marilyn and Jocelyn were grown, they began to handle more and more of the holiday dinners. Ada would hover around the kitchen to make sure everything was up to her standards. If it didn't add up in her mind, she'd nudge them and say, "Girl, I don't know about that!" This generally resulted in a round of laughter from all. Roles changed, but Ada was still the manager, driver, overseer and head of the kitchen – no matter what anyone thought.

Quitting Is Not an Option

Like others in this book, Marilyn was probably more reflective than introverted growing up. She was bestowed with many talents, including a studious, inquisitive mind. Learning still excites her.

Early in life she aspired to be a nun. She thought it was because she always had a heart for the church and not because of any personal tragedy in her life. She loved and felt the pull of God in her life and wanted to serve Him. That spiritual love has not changed over the years. But, at age nine, she gave up on the nun idea and turned to art. She would draw at every opportunity.

"I recall drawing the mermaid on the 'Chicken of the Sea' can over and over," says Marilyn. "I transitioned to writing in the tenth grade. Then, I shifted to poetry because it was a way to express how I saw the world."

As her interest changed, so did Marilyn's direction. She was fascinated with history and numbers were fun. Maybe a math or history teacher was her future. By her senior year, her interests had turned to psychology because maybe she could find the answers on why and how we viewed others. Ultimately, when a friend decided to go to DeVry Institute of Technology to become an engineer, Marilyn decided she had finally found her direction. She followed her friend into technology. It would take a few additional steps and/or missteps, but she would finally emerge with her Bachelor of Science degree later in life. It was in Economics/Finance!

Though Marilyn's interest changed over the years, she was always on the path of achieving and Ada was one of her biggest boosters. Ada encouraged Marilyn all the way. No matter what the dream or the desire, Ada wanted her children to be persistent and follow through.

But the path was not always rosy. Marilyn decided to join the band in the seventh grade. After one frustrating Friday in dealing with the band director, Marilyn wanted to quit the band. The director had a rule that if you were not in full uniform the morning of the Pep Rally, you could not participate at the football game. There were no exceptions. Marilyn was not at the Pep Rally; therefore, she would be sitting in the library, while the band was at the game. Marilyn knew exceptions had been made and she was furious with the band director when she couldn't justify her position. She felt the teacher was being unfair to her. She left school (with Ada's permission, of course) and came home and told her mother she wanted to quit the band.

"She looked at me and told me NO," says Marilyn. "Ada told me if I quit every time something in life wasn't fair, or when I had to work with people I didn't agree with, I would quit everything I did."

Of course, Marilyn didn't like that reasoning at all. However, when she became a mother herself, she understood better. Ada's PHD in motherhood proved insightful. It helped Marilyn through a failed marriage, raising a daughter (who is a teacher) and eventually completing her own education. There was no bigger cheerleader, when Marilyn received her Bachelor of Science degree in Economics/Finance, than Ada. It was the culmination of a lifelong goal and a day of celebration for Marilyn and Ada.

But Ada's advice didn't stop there. She continued to encourage Marilyn because she felt Marilyn was good with people. Though Ada has now passed on ... her words still encourage and push Marilyn to be and do more. That instinct to become a nun many years ago played out in many ways. Marilyn has gone on to get her master's degree in professional counseling and is still heavily tied to the church. She attended Seminary, as well. Per Marilyn, God and Ada continue to guide her life. Marilyn is now a proud grandmother of a beautiful baby boy, who we know will grow up with the wisdom passed down from Ada to Marilyn.

By the way, the band director did come by the house the following Saturday. He apologized and admitted he had made a mistake with his decision.

"He came by the house and won over my mother with a gallant gesture," steams Marilyn. "But all I could think at the time, when I saw him coming up the walk, was what was he doing at my house?"

"We often don't realize the sacrifices our mothers had to endure for us to be successful. I have been truly blessed by being raised by Ada. I daily am reminded of that strong, talented and undervalued woman who raised me," says 'The Professor.'

Linda Stone

LAZY IS NOT IN MY VOCABULARY

He who does not know to look where he came from will never get to his destination.
--Filipino Proverb

Slim, bespectacled with raven black hair, Erlinda (Linda) Stone is a consummate entrepreneur, teacher, coach and mentor. She is sincere, honest and giving of her time, information and support. It only takes a minute to understand that this woman is always busy. Perhaps part of it is her culture, which believes "laziness is the sibling of starvation." The rest is no doubt tied to lessons her mother taught her.

Linda, at one point, owned three businesses and provided formal mentoring and coaching to others. She is the CEO and Founder of APR Consulting, Inc., a staffing solution company providing talent, payroll services and vendor management for clients throughout the U.S. She also is the President and Founder of 24-Hour Medical Staffing Services, LLC, which provides healthcare professionals to hospitals, healthcare facilities and homes across the country. Linda co-founded another firm with a veteran partner called World Class Workforce Services, LLC. This firm specialized in training and counseling veterans and disabled veterans, then placing them in positions at client facilities.

I met Linda through the National Minority Supplier Development Council. She represented the Southern California area when I was the national chair representing minority businesses across the country. We have shared experiences over good meals and each time I learned something from Linda that has helped me in building my own businesses. Ever the coach and teacher, she once told me, "Terri, you just keep hiring managers and firing them until you finally get the one you want. You can't hold onto someone who doesn't fit the job." It sounded harsh, but her counseling has been helpful. It has forced me to place employees in the right position for their skill set and personality and then give them the tools they need to excel in their position.

Linda's lessons from her mother are numerous, but perhaps one of the biggest is "lazy is not a word in her vocabulary!"

Don't Just Sit There

Iluminada (Lumen) Reyes was all businesswoman, wife and mother. She raised nine children and was always working. She did not believe in sitting around. She was always busy. She specialized in buying products wholesale and selling them for profit. She sold clothing, handbags, jewelry, accessories and beauty products. She also helped her husband run

Linda Stone's father and mother (right), Iluminada (Lumen) Reyes (Linda was always the photographer)

his tailoring business. Lumen found the clients for the tailoring business, bought and sold the fabrics and managed the books. She bought the fabrics; her husband and staff made the suits, pants and shirts.

"My mom would always say 'If you want something bad enough, do not just sit there -- go get it,'" recalls Linda.

"Being lazy is not an option," was another 'momism' she offered us."

Linda clearly took this lesson to heart. She was a trained teacher before deciding to leave for a position with Corporate America. She climbed the corporate ladder in the Information Technology (IT) profession over an eight-year period before leaving to start her own IT consulting service. She grew APR Consulting into a very successful business but didn't let that stop her from looking for additional opportunities.

When she was diagnosed with breast cancer, she noticed there were shortages in the healthcare field for qualified healthcare professionals. "When I needed someone to look after me at home while I was recuperating," says Linda, "I couldn't find anyone to hire. I promised that when I survived cancer, I would start a nurse registry." She did. The nurse registry expanded into her 24-Hour Medical Staffing Services.

Each company has been wildly successful and has established Linda and her companies on the list of the most recognized and fastest growing in the country. Not being lazy and keeping an eye out for opportunities has been a successful lesson Lumen passed down to her daughter.

Linda noticed military personnel were coming back from war zones ready to work but unable to find good paying jobs to support their families. Again, believing you don't just sit there, Linda started a firm to cater primarily to veterans. Her partner was a Foreign War Veteran, who served as a medical doctor treating injured soldiers. They helped returning military personnel released from active duty by matching their experience, skills and education with the positions Linda's clients are wanted filled. This resulted in her third company – World Class Workforce Services.

Resilience

Unfortunately, business and life do not always go as planned.

"One of the virtues I inherited from my Mom is resilience," says Linda. "You never give up."

Linda's veteran partner in Word Class Workforce Services suffered from PTSD and had to be hospitalized. That worthwhile endeavor had to close.

She was back to managing two companies instead of three. When APR Consulting, Inc. lost its small business status, that meant losing its contract with an aerospace company. That represented 60% of the overall business. Linda didn't bemoan her position. She remembered the words of her mother and decided on a plan. She rallied her executive team and began to strategize to recuperate the lost revenue and to continue to remain as a medium size company. That required her and her team to reorganize, restructure, lay off employees and change the overall strategy. Despite this major setback, Linda and her team were able to remain a medium size company and build the growth momentum once again.

When Linda's husband passed away in April 2018, she was faced with another challenge. He was Chief Financial Officer for the companies and his passing left a huge hole. Linda had been planning to retire, but now she had to become both the CEO and CFO of her companies, as well as deal with the loss of her lifelong partner. Her plan to retire had to be postponed.

She once again rallied her troops – this time her three children. She began training them and delegating more responsibilities to them. Today, they play major roles in managing critical parts in the companies. Linda still owns and operates the two companies, but she is grooming her children to become CEOs and Presidents

"I am so proud that they took the responsibilities and are doing well. I hope to be able to retire in a year or maybe semi-retire and start another business," she laughingly offers.

<u>You Are Who You Want to Be</u>

"**I** was born and raised surrounded by poor families and hungry children," remembers Linda. "My life's ambition was to live a better life than those people and to be self-sufficient. I promised myself I would do everything in my power, so I would never raise hungry children."

Lumen used to tell her children that their fulltime job was to go to school and that her job and that of her husband was to make the necessary money to support the family. She wanted her children to understand that they should not let the world define or limit them. It was up to them to learn, grow and achieve.

"My mom would often tell us 'You are who you want to be. Do the best you can in everything you do,'" quotes Linda. Lumen practiced what she preached. She made sure her family got along well. She and her husband were a team. She was always on the go but managed to look like she enjoyed whatever she was doing. Even when she was tired, she never complained. She made sure she and her husband spent time on the weekends with the family. She made sure the family lived a balanced life.

"We did our chores on Saturday," recounts Linda. "We went to church on Sunday and then had Sunday outings. We celebrated holidays with the family, and my mom often entertained guests and relatives."

Lumen's legacy still lives on. Linda and her brothers and sisters still get together once a year in "The Family Gathering." They know they can count on each other when someone needs support and love.

Linda takes it a step further in following Lumen's footsteps. She mentors and coaches her son with his business, Enterprise Resource Services. In addition, she mentors and coaches the management team of her husband's business, 24-Hour Human Resource Outsourcing Services. "I share my lessons learned with them, so they can avoid pitfalls and position their company for success," says Linda.

Linda has not raised hungry children. In fact, she has been instrumental in helping her children and numerous others become what they want to be and achieve their dreams, as well.

Beatriz (Betty) Manetta

A WHIRLWIND FORCE

Mirror, Mirror on the wall,
I am my mother after all.
--Unknown

All it takes is a moment in her presence and you either come away exhausted or enthused. Her mind, talk and gestures all move at warp speed about her next idea. Whether it's something she thinks you should be doing, or how to fix an organization or company or how to use the next big technology discovery, Beatriz (aka Betty) Manetta is a whirlwind force to be reckoned with. I often call her the living, breathing "energizer bunny" because the only time she slows down is when she sleeps, and that is not for long.

72

Betty is an amazing entrepreneur in the true sense of the word. She is always thinking – she calls it continuous learning. She is an avid reader with a quick mind and strong technology understanding. She has parlayed her corporate and life experiences into two multi-million-dollar technology-driven companies – Argent Associates and Asociar -- that she continually adjusts to tackle the fast-changing tech environment. Argent Associates, her 20-year old baby, began as a logistics and Value-Added Reseller of network equipment for the telecommunications market. It has not only grown into a business that continues to offer network solutions, but also development of its own proprietary technology gateway and solutions. This technology can be used in numerous other marketplaces like energy, automotive, smart cities, as well as enhancing the customer experience and revenue-sharing opportunities for enterprises. Asociar is a leading network solutions company empowering connectivity for the world. With its emphasis on data center efficiencies, virtualized networks, 5G support and deployment, it is set to deliver the solutions needed to provide connectivity around the world.

Where does she get all that energy and drive? One might say it was inherited from her mother.

Creating a New World of Opportunities

Betty's mom, Berta Margarita Dominguez was born in Argentina. At a young age, she and her two brothers were orphaned after their father died. They were sent to an orphanage and separated from each other. Betty's great-grandmother and grandmother worked to get Berta and her brothers out of the orphanage. The women sewed leather books at a bindery during the day and cleaned for the rich and the military when not at the bindery – two jobs to hold family together. Eventually, grandmother married and was able to claim the children and reunite the family. By then the children had grown into teenagers.

Seated, Beatriz (Betty Manetta) and her sister Alicia Fitzpatrick, standing, her mom Berta Margarita Dominguez Donadio

Berta dropped out of grammar school to help her mother raise her newest brother. Evita Perone (yes, that Evita) gave the family something they could make money with – a sewing machine. Grandmother was able to sew curtains and returned to making books for the military.

Berta, however, never returned to school but continued to work. In due course, she went to work for the phone company in Argentina. It was there that Berta met Betty's father, Guillermo Lazaro Donadio.

Berta's family was German Jewish. Guillermo was Italian. He came from money and could trace his linage back to the Pope. Once the couple married, they lived with his family. Despite no formal education, Guillermo was a wiz at math and sketching. He worked in advertising and sketched for the newspaper. Betty and her older sister were born in Argentina, and the family continued to live with Betty's paternal grandmother.

When Betty was five, the family decided to leave Argentina. There was much political unrest in the country between the pro-Peron supporters, the military and the People's Radical Civil Union. Guillermo experienced his own troubles and thought it best to leave the country and move his family to the U.S. It was not an easy decision. They left the only home they knew, spoke no English and sought assistance from their church.

Betty tells one story about her family's experience in traveling by bus from Miami to their new home in Elizabeth, New Jersey. "We were on a bus, and my father spoke no English. A black woman got on the bus, and my father stood up to give her his seat. He was raised to be a gentleman because chivalry was the custom in Argentina. However, the white people on the bus began yelling at him. He didn't understand a word, and it almost caused a riot on the bus. He didn't understand that the laws of the South prevented blacks from sitting anywhere except in the back of the bus. One kind gentleman who happened to speak a little Spanish figured out my dad didn't understand what was going on. He quelled the situation and the woman moved to the back of the bus. We thought America was a very strange world and questioned whether it was a good idea to have left Argentina and family."

The family did make the journey safely on the bus and ended up living with a family in New Jersey. Although Elizabeth had its own racial tensions, it was nothing like their experience in the South. That experience helped establish Betty's long-term resolve and crusade regarding championing for diversity and the underserved.

Berta and Guillermo began looking for jobs, while they got the two girls enrolled in Catholic school. Because Berta's English and education were limited, she worked in the factories in Elizabeth NJ. This is where the family ended up settling. Berta worked at Fulton Sportswear and was part of the Women's Garment Workers Union. It was a Jewish sweatshop. When the factory closed, Berta went to work for Singers Sewing Machine Company, which made piece parts for the sewing machines. She would come home with her nails black from making bolts all day. They were paid by the piece, and the work had to be quality. Berta won awards for her quality work and number of pieces produced.

She worked two jobs. After working all day at Singers, she would come home, whip up a home-cooked meal for the family, check on the children and their homework and then head off to her janitorial job. She worked for a Portuguese janitorial company that had the contract cleaning airplanes. Berta had an abundance of energy and grit. At 4'11", she was a tremendous role model for her daughters. She walked fast, talked fast, cooked fast and cleaned fast. But, in each of those scenarios, she was always focused on helping her children achieve the American Dream. She knew education was the way, and every ounce of her being went into making sure they did well in school no matter what her sacrifices.

Berta continued her two jobs until the time Singers shut down its New Jersey plant and moved it to the Carolinas. Eventually, the plant went overseas. (Needless to say, the impact upon Betty's mother and the family when Singers shut down further solidified Betty's views on keeping jobs in the U.S.A. and the role of businesses and their corporate social responsibilities.)

Eventually, when Betty married and had her first child Michael, Berta retired, and Betty encouraged her to live with them and take care of her grandson. Berta acquiesced and retired from working outside the home to enjoy her final years relishing her grandson.

Drive, speed, energy, integrity, love and cooking are all the wonderful experiences and lessons Berta passed on to Betty. I have had the pleasure of getting to know Betty over the years, and we each have shared many tales about our childhood and growing up experiences. I can clearly see the imprint of Berta on Betty, but here are just a few tales that demonstrate the love that has passed from generation to generation. (Oh yeah, one of those shared experiences is tearing up at the mention of our mothers and how much they meant to us.)

More Jobs. More Money.

One thing Betty clearly learned from Berta was that if you wanted to have more money, you needed to go out and get more jobs. Betty believed in the American Dream her mother sought for her and her siblings. Lack of money would not quell her dreams. Energy and focus could make them happen. Betty has had a long list of jobs growing up including bartender (she still makes great mixed drinks and knows her wine), driving an ice cream truck, selling t-shirts and beer at the Englishtown Raceway and even running a construction company. When her daughter came along and wanted to learn ballet and dance, Betty started a non-profit dance company. Just like Berta, Betty often worked two jobs and got both her degrees while working full-time. She received a Bachelor of Science degree in Accounting and Marketing from Rutgers University and her Master of International Study from Seaton Hall University.

Betty would work for AT&T (the Bell System) for 20 years with positions in human resources, sales, technical support, quality control and management and international sales. Before she left AT&T, she held the position of Director of International Sales in the Middle East and later Latin America.

In all those assignments and opportunities, she would never forget the lessons of energy, hard work and education that Berta instilled in her.

Actions Have Consequences

Another hard lesson Betty learned from her parents was them letting her deal with the consequences of her own actions. Though now a funny story that Betty is not too proud to share, I am sure it was not funny at the time. As mentioned earlier, her parents worked very hard to send her and her siblings to a Catholic School. It was not cheap, and they made many sacrifices to make sure their children were instilled with faith, respect and a good education. Like all youngsters, however, Betty probably didn't take all that too seriously at the time. After all, wasn't that what parents are supposed to do?

Betty had been chosen class president, co-captained the cheerleading squad and was quite popular in school. However, one day during her senior year, she was caught in the bathroom with some girls who were smoking. Betty had been warned more than once with a threat to kick her out of school the next time she was caught. Three strikes and you're out! This time, Betty was not actually smoking. She just happened to be hanging out with those who were. When they heard the nun approaching the bathroom, they hid the cigarettes. One was located where Betty was sitting, and she was kicked out of school.

Having to tell her parents was probably one of the hardest things she had to do as a teenager. And, because it was her senior year, she had to decide what to do next. She just couldn't sit at home and get the kind of jobs she needed.

These kinds of jobs were not going to get her where she wanted to be long term. Plus, all her friends would think she was a real loser.

She dusted off her pride and enrolled in the public school, where she had the "wonderful" experience of being the new kid on the block who happened to look like a white girl. She accepted the responsibility for her actions and ended up graduating from the public high school.

"It all worked out," said Betty. "Today, I now celebrate two high school reunions and have close friends from both schools."

In another test of her will, she returned from pregnancy leave after having her daughter Lia, only to find out there was no job. Corporate downsizing left her with no corporate option. That propelled her into establishing Argent Associates in her basement, using her pool table as her conference room and desk. She went to her previous boss and asked for the opportunity to bid on some of the projects. The answer was yes. With no money, no employees and no real business, she used her connections and understanding of the projects to place her first bids. She won, and one of her old suppliers in her previous world would help mentor and back her in her new world. The rest, they say, is history. Argent Associates not only won but has succeeded in being recognized as one of the leading women and Hispanic-owned companies in the nation.

Cooking as An Elixir

I am not so sure Berta would consider cooking as a relaxing tonic for all that ails you because it was a necessity for her way of life. However, it is clear from Betty that her mom enjoyed cooking and was a wonderful chef. They were far away from their family and friends in Argentina, but Berta always stayed in contact with them and through the food helped her children appreciate their heritage.

Argentine cuisine is described as a cultural blending of Mediterranean influences. Thus, it's not a surprise if you visit Betty and her family that she is constantly whipping up amazing Italian (she, too, married into an Italian family just like Berta). She loves to cook, entertain and try new dishes. Even though she knows nothing about sports (maybe she doesn't care to know), she hosts huge Super Bowl parties and Yankee-watching events at her home with husband Bob. Fine wines are served with constantly appearing appetizers and entrees made of shrimp, lobster, fresh peppers, olives, breads, pastas, sausages and more and more and more!

Plus, when she is at her home in Plano, Texas (she has two homes – one in New Jersey and one in Texas), she is continually trying new dishes out on her employees. It seems every Monday, the kitchen at work is filled with some of Betty's culinary delights.

Not lost in all this is Betty's connection, collaboration and enjoyment with people from all walks of life. Her quick and inquisitive mind is continually challenging, absorbing and assimilating data and information about people, projects and opportunities to expand her life, her business and her loves.

A Giving Heart and Soul

I couldn't leave talking about Betty Manetta without talking about her unbelievable giving nature. It's how we met and why we have become such good friends. She is unpretentious, and if you can get past that New Jersey passion and speech, you'll find a soft and giving heart that engulfs everyone she meets – especially the less fortunate. Back to the experience on the bus, Betty has taken that experience full circle. She has helped young women understand the requirements to be successful in the corporate world and as an entrepreneur. She supports all things STEM (Science, Technology, Engineering, Mathematics) for women and minorities. She has hired and educated her warehouse workers, who are now proficient technologists and software developers. She has lived up to the *Made in the U.S.A.* brand and turned the mantra into one of the key values of her companies. Her workforce is reflective of how America really looks. And... she has won numerous awards being herself!

Smart, confident, giving and energetic – Betty is all the things Berta would have her to be and more!

Marie Diaz

FINDING BEAUTY THROUGH THE ASHES

I've learned that when God promises beauty through the ashes, He means it.

– Taya Kyle

Marie Diaz is a highly successful entrepreneur who has parlayed her people skills, tenacity and pursuit of excellence into a multi-million-dollar business empire. She is the CEO and Chief Visionary Officer of Pursuit of Excellence, a human resources firm focused on organizational development and design, training, benefits professionals development and establishing smarter business protocols for business enterprises. In addition, she is a successful author of a book entitled *If You Knew You*

Could Not Fail, What Would You Do? (In Survival, There is No Choice) and is working on a second book entitled *Faith Leadership*. She is a sought-after speaker on leadership, strategy, human resource solutions and entrepreneurship, who has offices around the world ("I thought it made sense to have offices where I like to visit, so that's what I did," chuckles Marie).

As an entrepreneur, she lives by a personal motto: "Success doesn't come to you, you go to it." Marie says, "Although today, others may say that I am a shining example of what persistence and dedication can bring, my business accomplishments are intrinsically linked to a long and difficult journey. When the odds were against me, I found myself with only one option—rise to the occasion and make something happen. I became an expert at that skill and placed it at the core of my personal survival and career. It's up to you to build your future and your story just the way you want it to be."

Marie 's early story is like too many in our nation – raised by destructive men and a loving mother, poor but still hopeful and determined to live a better life than her parents. Marie's rise through the ashes to experience the beauty and success of today is a formidable tale. We provide just a glimpse into how the mother that raised her had such a tremendous impact on her adult life and direction.

Find Sunshine in The Struggles

Marie's mother, Virginia Ramirez

Virginia Ramirez was born and raised in San Antonio, Texas. She married at sixteen and had three children soon after. Marie was the middle child with an older and younger brother. Virginia did not work outside the home and lived in an abusive marriage with an alcoholic husband who wasn't faithful to his vows. He was killed, leaving Virginia widowed with three children when Marie was just three years old.

Virginia married once again only to continue the cyclical pattern of an alcoholic husband. He was in the military and became Marie's stepfather. The family moved to Dallas when Marie was in the second grade. In Dallas, Virginia began working outside the home. The job gave her some independence and a whole new view of what her world could be. It wasn't long before she decided to get divorced and stay single. She could do it on her own and worked two to three jobs to keep her family safe and fed.

It was Virginia who helped her daughter Marie understand dreams did not need to be confined to current circumstances. Virginia quietly encouraged her daughter to reach higher and envision herself achieving. She could do that by being focused on her dreams. Virginia couldn't afford expensive things or vacations with her children, but she did teach them to imagine a better world for themselves. She loved visiting estate sales and told Marie to pretend they were on a vacation visiting a really nice place. Together they would peruse the expensive items people had bought and were selling. These visits gave Marie a peek into the world of beauty and wonderful things. She learned to dream of the possibilities for her life and not accept less for her future.

Virginia kept her dreams alive as well. She started a beauty salon in the poor area of town, while the family lived with their grandmother. By then, Marie was a working woman herself. Virginia helped Marie with the kids and Marie helped fund the beauty parlor. After all, poor people deserve to be beautiful too!

The Big Decision

As Marie experienced more success in her career, she found herself traveling away from her kids constantly. By then, she was a single mother with three young boys. She would be gone three weeks out of the month and away from her sons. She had a live-in nanny, but that was doing nothing for the relationship between her and her boys. In fact, she figured she needed the boys more than they needed her at this point.

She came home one day after 22 hours of working and traveling from Australia and found that the key to her front door didn't work. She panicked. What had happened to her children and the nanny? What was going on in her life? Once the nanny opened the door, Marie found her furniture had been rearranged and there was cooking going on in the kitchen. She was livid. Who decided to change her home? When the dust settled, there was a rational explanation for everything. The nanny had lost the keys, so she had the locks changed. The boys had rearranged the furniture and were cooking a surprise welcome home meal in the kitchen. Once Marie calmed down, she overheard the nanny mumble something about this being Marie's house, but she (the nanny) was the one who lived in it. This incident ended the relationship and Marie's long travels away from home.

Shortly thereafter, Marie would make the big decision to change the course of her life. After firing the nanny, she decided to create her own business. She had built a business network, she had the skills and knowledge in human resources, and she figured she could create a successful business out of what she knew best (Isn't that how most entrepreneurs get started?). If it failed, she could always get another job. Plus, this would give her the chance to reacquaint herself with her boys. Pursuit of Excellence, Inc. was born.

The Challenge Begins

Virginia died of an aneurysm during the first year of Marie's business. It was sudden and devastating for Marie. Virginia was only 43. She had been the leading motivator and supporter for Marie and her dreams. It was hard to move on without her.

But that wasn't the only challenge that hit during the first few years of business. Marie was involved in a major car accident that left her unable to walk for almost a year. She had numerous surgeries and had to have her ankle broken three times before it would be set to heal correctly. It was after that third surgery that Marie started cold calling and making appointments. What else was there to do? She made it to her first appointment – in heels, no less! Mental toughness and true grit continued to define Marie's life and her direction.

Twenty plus years later, Pursuit of Excellence is a multi-million-dollar business providing human resources services and solutions. In addition, Marie started several businesses related to things she loves – food and wine and bringing leaders together. She is the proud founder of CEO Clubs of Australia, Cielo Bistro and soon to come NOVA – a Fine Mexican Cuisine restaurant. Marie is a frequent keynote speaker for business and community organizations. She is considered a thought leader and an expert in her field. She advocates for young adults in the pursuit of leadership and entrepreneurship.

Marie has applied her entrepreneurial determination, persistence, continuous improvement and learning through failure to help inspire and motivate corporate executives, business entrepreneurs and individuals. She seeks to help others aspire to achieve a higher degree of professional and personal success.

Author's mom, Doris Marie Lovejoy (circa 50's)

NOT ALL ROSES

She stood in the storm, and when the wind did not blow her away, she adjusted her sails.

--Elizabeth Edwards

Everything about my Mom's life was not a bed of roses despite growing up around a network of supportive family and friends. From an early age, she was her own independent thinker. Some might have called it stubbornness. She graduated from a country high school at age 16. By the time she was 17, she was married and pregnant with my older brother. She and the city boy she married had a difficult time – two young, headstrong kids trying to know each other, work and raise their son. By the time my mom reached 20 she had had enough of the struggle. Divorce was imminent. However, when she planned to move back home with my older brother in tow, my grandmother convinced her to give the marriage one more try. She did … and oops! Along came me – Terri Lee Henderson or Terri Lee, as my mother often called me. She was now 21. Her stubborn nature knew what it knew. This marriage would not endure. She finally divorced and moved back to the country with TWO children now instead of one.

A New Start

Starting over, Mom did the only thing she knew how to do -- she stayed with her parents, got a job cleaning houses and my grandmother watched over my brother and me. Cleaning up after the wealthy was not a new story for my family or other black women. It was the tradition of my grandmother and my great aunts. It is what they knew how to do. They were good at cleaning houses, taking in ironing and occasionally watching someone else's children. The city was full of wealthy women in need of domestic help. It was the capital of Kansas and the Menninger Clinic had made a name for itself treating wealthy, mentally-disturbed people. Well-off families in need of domestic help seemed plentiful.

My mom simply entered the "family business" and began to build a new life for her children and herself.

Doris Marie was still young and quite "the looker." On weekends, she'd go out on the town with her two cousins. (All three were only months apart in age. People often thought they were sisters because they traveled everywhere together.). On one of those outings she met a young man who dressed nicely, had his own automobile and owned part of a struggling black-owned cab company. He was from Chicago, or so he said. He'd been injured in WWII and shipped to the V.A. in Topeka for rehabilitation from his wounds. One of his partners in the service was from the area, so he decided to stay in Topeka a while and try and make a home. He too was a divorcee. His name may have said it all…Love – joy – Lawrence Lovejoy!

Author's parents - Doris and Lawrence Lovejoy

The two kept company. The young man told my mom she was too smart to just be cleaning houses. He asked her why she didn't go back to school. His cab company was faltering because "black folks always want to travel free," he said. (In this day and age, it would be explained as a "hookup." Everyone wanted a free or discounted cab ride!) He had decided to go to trade school and learn to lay bricks and repair houses instead. My mom listened to him and decided to take his advice and go to secretarial school.

I was three when she first brought him home. My mom tells the story that I chose this man as my Daddy even before my mom said yes. When this slick city boy drove up to the country home, I was wrapped in dirt and had sand all over me because I had been playing in the tire sandbox on the front of the driveway. I saw the man get out of his shiny and waxed car. I threw down whatever I was playing with and ran toward him yelling "Daddy! Daddy!" To his credit he picked me up, held me at arms' length so I wouldn't dirty his pressed and clean swank suit and proceeded toward my grandparent's back door. My grandmother saw him with me and came running. She snatched me out of his arms telling me, "That's not your daddy!" But I got the last laugh. Mom ended up marrying the young man (despite protestations from my grandparents). And I was blessed to call him my daddy!

Mom made a career as a clerk typist for the State of Kansas. She was good, bright, quick and an exceptional administrator -- ordering and giving directions. Together the couple built a home (literally), raised five children and were married for over 45 years.

She sometimes struggled raising my younger brothers, especially when my dad's job was transferred from Topeka to Oklahoma City. She didn't want to leave the home they had built or the cocoon of her parents, so she stayed in Topeka, while he commuted from Oklahoma City. Today, that type of marriage is not uncommon. Servicemen did it all the time. My dad worked at Tinker Airforce Base inspecting parts for fighter planes.

Raising a family with three young boys and an intermittent father could tax even the most stalwart of people. Money was tight trying to manage two homes across two states, but they managed to make it work. As with all things in her life, she made a decision and just tackled the consequences head on. They found time for family vacations to Houston and Chicago. Mom took time away and went to Oklahoma City to be with Dad. And he came home as often as he could, even driving on ice-slicked roads in the wintertime just to be home for the holidays. They made it work.

On her job, racism raised its ugly head. She met it head on as best she could. It prevented her quick wit and brains from being used to its fullest on the job. She was passed over many times for a full secretarial job, not awarded the raises she deserved and continually trained new bosses to do their job. It didn't stop her from trying to better herself. She took tests, studied shorthand and continued to improve her skills. By the time she retired, she and the others in the department knew she "ran" everything, though she never was rewarded with the pay or the position.

Mom compensated by engrossing herself into creating a world of love and protection for her children. Sometimes, like everyone, life was good to her and sometimes not. But she never let it hinder who she was and what she thought of herself or her family.

I don't know if she ever had second thoughts about her choices. (Having been married myself, I am sure she did.) She made this second marriage stick for her children, her husband and herself. She created a strong family bound by love and laughter that has endured through the generations.

She encouraged us all to go to college. Get a good education. Get a good job. She told us, "You can be whatever you want to be." Whether that was true or not, we believed her. I believed her. Like everyone else, I have experienced obstacles in my life, but I fully recognize I can't control anyone but myself and I make every effort to do my best.

If mothers ruled the world.... what a world this would be!

To describe my mother would be to write about a hurricane in its perfect power. Or the climbing, falling colors of a rainbow.

— *Maya Angelou*

PART 3 - Vegan Grits

Education commences at the mother's knee, and every word spoken within hearsay of little children tends toward the formation of character.

--Hosea Ballou

*Education has always been touted by the less fortunate as the avenue to a better life. The mothers in this book were no different. Not all had the chance to attend school and found the privilege of their children being able to do so like finding the Holy Grail. It delivered a path to a better life and more opportunities, and they would not let their children know or think otherwise. This chapter entitled, **Vegan Grits**, takes education a step further. It reminds us all to never stop learning and striving. Whether vegan or gluten-free or keto is your thing, there is always something new around the corner to experience. Why not **Vegan Grits?***

Avis Yates Rivers

REFLECTING EXCELLENCE

Be a Mother who is committed to loving her children into standing on higher ground than the environment surrounding them

— *Marjorie Pay Hinckley*

Naturally coiffed red hair, a wide inviting smile and dark black-brown receptive eyes sit atop a chocolate brown, fit body. She's a New Yorker and it doesn't take long in her presence to hear the accent, the occasional rapid-fire speaking when she's excited and a readiness to take on the world! She is New York through and through – though not the obnoxious representative of the region. She's more

99

engaging, welcoming and affable. She is a lady you can readily call sister because she makes those around her feel comfortable and at home in her presence. Whether she is promoting her business (something constantly at the forefront of her demeanor) or making the rounds at a major event, connecting with those she knows or wants to know, Avis Yates Rivers is in-sync with her surroundings and her life's purpose. Spiritual, driven and friendly, she looks and feels fit in mind, body and soul.

I met Avis as a part of the National Minority Supplier Development Council. I was a newly elected representative for the North Texas chapter, and she was a Regional Chair out of the New York/New Jersey area. At our introduction, she turned to my predecessor and mentor, Charles Griggsby and said, "Oh, so they do have women leaders in Texas!" It was the kind of insight into the good ole boys' network that endeared her to me. Avis became a mentor to a new female representative from Georgia and me. We listened and learned all about the network, diversity and leadership from Avis. She took us under her wings and showed us the ropes of leading, achieving and impacting events for the betterment of minority business inclusion. Over the ensuing years, she also showed us how to gracefully exit the leadership limelight and move on to bigger and different quests. (Perhaps some athletes could use her help in this area!)

Avis is the President and CEO of Technology Concepts Group International (TCGI), an Information Technology (IT) asset management and full-service equipment leasing firm. Her hard work as an IT solutions provider proved fortuitous when Bank of America sought to spin-off its leasing division. Avis and TCGI had worked with Bank of America for many years and when the opportunity arose in 2008, Avis seized it. She weathered the "Great Recession" and has grown TCGI into a strong, expanding company with a variety of corporate clients nationwide. Her entrepreneurial spirit, seasoned by her mother's example, is topped with a dash of striving for excellence in all that she does.

Do Your Best

Annie Toliver with daughter Avis Rivers Yates

Annie Toliver was born the oldest girl of six children – three boys and three girls. She grew up in Greenville, South Carolina in the mid-30's, when Jim Crow and the South sought to set limits on what a young black child could achieve. Annie's mother, however, believed in raising her children with a firm hand and taught Annie to follow her lead. Annie had no formal education; she was married at the age of fifteen. She and her husband, a minister, moved to Augusta, GA early in their marriage. There, a son and daughter, Avis, were born. The family relocated to New York City when Avis was just one. Like many southerners at the time, the promise of better jobs and improved living conditions beckoned the young family northward.

The family settled in New York City. Annie went to work as a laborer in a watch factory. Her husband worked and attended graduate school to obtain his degrees in the ministry. Three more children followed Avis in close succession. The young girl became caretaker for her younger siblings while her mom and dad worked.

Annie, however, was always actively engaged in the lives of her children. She encouraged them to be prepared in school and work.

"Don't hand in just anything to the teacher," admonished Annie. "It needs to be the very best you can do." She stressed excellence and encouraged them to do their best always. She expected her children to look good, to be positive no matter what life threw at them and to be dignified. The way Annie saw it, how one's children looked and behaved reflected on the parents. "She expected all of her children to look good, act respectful and strive to be excellent in all they did," remembers Avis.

Of course, anyone who has met Avis knows she took these lessons to heart. Always a fashionable standout, you can hear the gravelly voice, turn around, and see a well put together woman crossing the room engaged in conversation. Her confidence, her demeanor and her positive outlook on life, regardless of the circumstances, are winning ways in the world of Avis Yates Rivers.

"My mother believed in excellence," recalls Avis. "She made sure we were prepared for school. We had to carry ourselves with dignity and always look clean and presentable. My mother said the way you carry yourself reflects on who you are."

Early on, Avis thought she wanted to be a teacher. She had a ready classroom using her younger siblings and often played school with them. She was the teacher and she expected her sibling students to listen, learn and obey her every direction. (This might have been her entree into public speaking; she was a natural). Avis also was a voracious reader when she was young. Her inquisitive mind (still a major part of her persona) soaked up all kinds of information found in books – travel, new ideas, history and more. Her insatiable desire to learn no doubt set her course to achieve in the field of technology – an exciting, ever-changing environment and industry. (She was STEM – Science, Technology, Engineering, and Mathematics – before most knew how to spell the acronym.)

Avis was educated in the public schools of New York City. Ever mindful of Annie's push for excellence and "don't just hand in anything" philosophy, Avis was successful in matriculating through the school system. By the time she was in high school, her parents had bought Cherry Value Dairy, a convenience store. Avis worked at the store after school and on the weekends while going to high school at the same time. It was hard work, and it was during these times she learned to appreciate that owning something meant hard work to make it successful. She had opportunities upon graduation to leave the area to go to school. She chose to stay close to home, where the tuition was free, and she could work and go to school. She stayed in New York and attended the City University of New York.

Upon graduation from college with her Business of Administration degree, Avis went to work for Exxon. She had interned at the company while in college and was hired permanently upon graduation. She worked in various divisions, getting a rounded view of the company and corporate America. The last five years at Exxon were spent in the Office Automation Services division, which sold technology solutions to businesses. Her territory included Wall Street. It was in this assignment that Avis found her niche. She learned to talk and sell technology to businesses of all sizes. When Exxon decided to sell the division, Avis figured it was time for her to step out on her own. In 1985, she launched her first business out of her house. During the first two years of the new company's existence, Exxon was one of her top clients.

An Abiding Care for Others

Annie not only provided guidance to her children related to work and school, she was also a leader in their spiritual development. Raised in the South and married to a minister, she wanted to ensure her children's successes included a spiritual component. No one was better than anyone else, and all needed help and assistance at some point. No one got to where they were alone. Family and spiritual guidance was important to Annie. The Lord is an important component in success. Annie also strongly believed in blessing others with her time and talents.

"My mother accomplished a lot as a young bride," says Avis. "She married at age 15 and without a formal education she raised very successful children. She instilled a love of the Lord in all of us."

Avis is an active leader in her church home. She is the mother of four children and six grandchildren. She and her husband have returned to her family's roots -- South Carolina. They now make their home at Hilton Head. Family has always been important to her. Her grandmother lived until she was 101 and Annie seems to be going strong, even today. Avis remains close to her mom and family members. That support system and close connection is as much a part of Avis as it is to Annie.

Avis also shares herself and her talents with others. A committed advocate for minority and women business inclusion in the economy, Avis is a ready conference speaker and facilitator on the subject. She has won numerous awards and recognition for her commitment to inclusion. In addition, she is adamant about including more girls and women in technology fields. She was recognized by the White House as a Champion of Change in STEM.

Avis' abiding faith continues to lead her to further heights. She still is an active member and leader in the church, and we are sure no one could be prouder of all her endeavors than her own mother, Annie. As a reflection of where she came from and her people, Annie is smiling about the excellent reflection her daughter represents of the family started in South Carolina!

Pamela Johnson Betts

SHE'S A LADY...

As is the mother, so is her daughter.
--Ezekiel 16:4

Dramatic, striking, confident, humble, engaging, put together ... comfortable in her own skin. All of these describe Pamela Johnson Betts. She is her own person with her own way of doing things – usually the "right" way. What you notice first about her is her outfits, her poise, her carriage. She is a lady! She was a "fashionista" before they even coined the word. She never wears the same outfit twice and she's an avid shopper who can put the simplest things together to create "the look." She has a beautiful face (inherited from her mother), with eyes, complexion and smile that needs little, if any makeup to accentuate her presence.

But don't think it's all about her – it is not! She is a walking contradiction – a fashion guru for certain, but she has spent her life in the service of others. She is one of the most giving, caring people I know.

I met Pamela in high school, and we have been sisters ever since. We struck up a friendship in Mrs. Shelton's English Literature class. I was considered the smart one and she was the pretty one. (She would never say she was pretty, though!) We both were just our own persons – opinionated, self-assured and private. We had a common bond of strong black mothers who nurtured and pushed us to be the best we could be. Pam is an only child, and I was the only girl in a houseful of brothers. There was a natural bond which has lasted despite distance, years and circumstances. We learned to not depend upon others to determine our happiness, our direction or even our limits. We lived in the world our mothers created where anything and everything was possible for their daughters. But of course, that's part of the story of lessons Pam's mother taught her!

Ever a Lady

Leslie Gardenhire Johnson was number seven of thirteen children who grew up on a small farm in Alma, Kansas, just outside of Topeka. For some reason, she was her maternal grandmother's favorite and was doted on by her. Perhaps, it was because they were so much alike. It was at her grandmother's knee Leslie learned an appreciation for wonderful and gracious things – clothing, recipes and

Young Pamela and her mom,
Leslie Gardenhire Johnson

entertaining. Her formal education stopped at high school, but she never stopped learning. She taught her only child, Pamela, the importance of thinking for herself; acting with style and grace; and being happy in her own skin.

Leslie knew how to do all three of these. She was a fun and funny lady, now restricted by age. She worked as an LPN, serving others throughout her career. On occasion, she worked at locations where her older sister and brother also worked. Other times she was on her own.

Leslie was always a lady. She dressed comfortably for work and at home, but she knew how to pull together an outfit when the occasion called for it. She enjoyed getting dressed in gowns, gloves and shoes to go out with her husband, C.O. (affectionately known as "Baby" by all who knew him). They were a cute couple.

"She taught me it is important to have style and grace with a carriage that includes physically and metaphorically holding the chin high," says Pamela about her mother. She adds, "It demonstrates an awareness of a backbone."

"She taught me the importance of knowing how to use language and the power a good communicator can command," continues Pamela. "And strength of character, values and the courage of your convictions as the real measures of a successful life; not possessions, the position you hold or the amount of money you have."

Pamela has spent her life living her convictions, commanding respect and ensuring respect for others. She is a trained social worker who has helped make the lives of children and the elderly better. In her early years, you could find her giving hard love to a parent whose child needed direction and discipline. Later in her career, she could be found patiently listening to an elderly person living in a nursing home in her role as Secretary of Aging for the State of Kansas. She helped to improve conditions and services. What better way to understand and make changes than to talk with the people in the home? When my dad was in the last stages of Alzheimer's, one of the facilities Pamela visited was the one he was in. He didn't know who she was, but my family and I were grateful for her visit to the home.

Though officially "retired" from public service, Pamela cannot sit still. Today, she is the Executive Director of the Topeka Public Schools District Foundation. Her work is designed to give children a better chance at a good education along with expanded life experiences. For some time, she did this all while taking care of her elderly mom. Service to others is and has been her life.

Self-Contented

Leslie learned to get along with others early in life. Growing up with twelve siblings on a farm doesn't require you to reach out much to meet others. However, it teaches you the skills necessary to build friendships navigate confusion and find inner peace. Leslie enjoyed the company of her husband and entertained both family and friends throughout her life.

She taught her daughter not to seek happiness from others. "Happiness, just like beauty, is something that comes from within us," Leslie imparted to her daughter.

Pamela recalls, "From my earliest recollection as an only child, she encouraged me to play outside or to read. Reading is still my most relaxing and rewarding endeavor. I am capable of easily entertaining myself. I enjoy my own company and am quite content not belonging to every social group or having my social calendar filled." Pam further relates how she was filled with joy when she used to hear her youngest son laughing out loud in his room, without another living soul with him. He, too, had learned the satisfaction of "self-contentment." Pam has passed that gift onto the next generation. It's a lesson what will serve him well.

Contentment leads to trusting your own judgment. You can stand strong for your beliefs. Life is not fair, and things don't always go your way; however, Leslie believed you must be strong through it all. Her life was not always easy. She and her husband lived apart for part of the week, because his job was in Kansas City and hers was in Topeka. Long before the days when two-career families made the headlines, Leslie and her husband, Charles, dealt with the reality of creating a better world for their daughter despite the challenges of living part of the week in two separate cities. They built a house, a home and surrounded Pamela with all the love and direction they knew how to give.

"My mom mastered the art of flexibility and instilled in me its importance in relationships and life," says Pamela. "To this day, I remain determined and when necessary can shift gears, pick myself up and move on to the next opportunity life has to offer."

Family, Fun and Soul Food

Holidays, birthdays and Sundays were all a time for family, fun and food at the Johnson household. Chatter filled the air. The family indulged in favorite family recipes. Around the table, each member was able to exchange thoughts, ideas and jokes. Laughter was on the menu and Leslie was often at the forefront of keeping things funny and upbeat. Her delicious food covered the table and she was the "hostess with the mostest."

Pamela Johnson Betts (center standing) with her family. Seated, her late mom, Leslie Gardenhire Johnson, late dad, Charles O. Johnson. Standing, from left to right, son Blake, Pamela, her late son Chaz and son Brandt

Leslie believed a loving family was important and nothing should stand in its way. It's a family-first philosophy that has been passed down to the next generations. She loved others unconditionally and taught her daughter to do the same. Pamela says, "Having faith in God and the pursuit of happiness began regularly by gathering the family around a table of delicious home-cooked family favorite recipes. It was a time to not only celebrate the birthday, holiday or one's accomplishments, but to thank God for the blessings He continually bestowed upon us."

Pamela has now taken over the role of hostess. The joy and task of preparing and hosting the family gatherings has been delegated to her. The family still enjoys eating, laughing and spending time with each other. Until her passing, Leslie remained the center of attention. She aged (gracefully, by the way) and faced the challenges of aging with aplomb and grittiness. Her kind, simple, humble, fun and funny personality shone through each uphill battle. She spoke highly of her daughter and her daughter continues to speak honor and respect the lessons she learned. Now a grandmother, herself, Pamela delights in the company of her family and enjoys those famous holiday and family meals. Thoughts of Leslie are not far from the gatherings.

Patricia Rodriguez Christian *A young Manuela Rodriguez:*
Patricia's mother

DEVIL IN THE DETAILS

Geeks are people who love something so much that all details matter.

--*Marissa Meyer*

At first, you don't realize she's really a "geek." You must get to know her to recognize the signs. Outwardly, she's striking. She's tall -- 5' 10", formerly with a mane of black hair (lost to a battle with cancer but growing back quickly) surrounding a face accented by striking chocolate eyes. She is all Hispanic in every good sense of the culture -- talented, smart, bi-lingual, self-assured and proud. She is Patricia Rodriguez Christian. She has defined her world, conquered her first-generation circumstances and stayed engaging and down to earth. She is a walking contradiction

115

– conservative in business yet liberal in social causes; introverted but engaging; guarded yet generous. In truth, she is a very private person who is cautious in declaring friends and/or confidences. Put in the right one-on-one or a small circle of people, she is full of insightful thoughts, witty conversation and nerdy tidbits.

Her interests range from art, to travel, to science and more. She is ever learning, ever providing strange facts that even I find amusing. And her mind truly does navigate toward the details of a situation. Whether we're talking contracts, profit and loss, marketing or personnel, she has a thought. Usually, it's a good one!

Patricia and I met while being a part of the Dallas/Fort Worth Minority Business Council (an organization dedicated to connecting minority-owned businesses with corporate and public agency buyers). When I was first introduced to her, I readily recognized talent and recruited her to be part of a leadership team I chaired. Since then, we have developed a friendship and a business partnership that continues to grow and open new doors.

Patricia is a serial entrepreneur. She owns CRC Group, and is a principal with me in ADP-LLC. But she has owned a floral shop, a restaurant, a real estate firm and numerous other businesses singularly and with her husband, Larry. She recently took over the leadership of her husband's construction company – Texas Standard Construction. She does all this while raising a teenage son – a clone of his mother and her brothers -- and battling through a health crisis. Did you know lipstick contains pig fat? It's a fact Marcus delighted in passing along to me when he was just five years old.

What did Patricia learn from her mother? The lessons include the "family business," a thirst for learning and self-assurance, as a start.

Self-Assurance

Manuela (far left) on the cattle ranch in Mexico.

Manuela Rodriguez was born in Mexico. She was the youngest of eleven children (there was a 22-year gap between her and her oldest sibling). She grew up on a cattle ranch close to the U.S. border. When Manuela's mother died, Manuela ran the family cattle ranch. With just a third-grade education, she raced horses, supervised the ranch hands and managed the ranch. There were always fresh vegetables, fruits and beef.

"It was kind of like 'Little House on the Prairie,'" Patricia says. "I am sure it wasn't all that great, but my mom seemed to thrive as the young woman in charge."

Manuela was engaged to be married in Mexico but decided that wasn't the life for her. Women had no rights and she was too liberal and independent to be saddled down with a man who might not appreciate her spirit. After all, she had seen the ranch hands and relatives interact with women and wanted no part of a submissive, obedient role. Instead, she decided to move to the States.

For a while, Manuela lived in New Mexico with her sisters. Her sisters were much older than her and were born in the U.S. before the Mexico border was redefined. In the U.S., Manuela worked as a nanny and helped raise her own nieces and nephews. She grew into who she was and what she wanted out of life before she finally decided to marry.

Manuela had met a young man who was in the U.S. on a guest workers program, and she wanted to be assured she would remain in the U.S. before she agreed to marry him. "Mom told my dad that she would only marry him if he could assure her she would remain in the States," said Patricia.

Manuela also told her daughter, "Do not ever be dependent upon a man. Be your own woman and decide for yourself what you want and who you want to be."

Patricia followed this advice. She waited to marry and began her life as independent and self-assured as her mother had advised her. She traveled, worked in New Mexico, Washington D.C. and then Dallas before deciding to "settle down" at the ripe old age of 33. She maintains her independent, self-assurance with the love of her entrepreneurial husband, Larry and young son, Marcus.

The Family Business

"I don't remember a time when my mom was not selling something," says Patricia. "We lived in the barrio and Mom was always selling items to the ladies – towels, sheets, rugs, winter coats, cleaning products, beauty products. If there was a need, she discovered where to get it and sold it to the women."

Patricia describes how her mom set up payment plans for the ladies. Each week, with Patricia in tow, she would pay a visit to collect payments and deliver goods. Manuela would offer what the marketplace was looking for at a fair price plus delivery service.

Patricia kept the books, read the supplier contracts and managed the payment plans – all at the ripe old age of ten! Patricia was bi-lingual and could manage negotiations in English with certain suppliers, as well as talk with the women in Spanish. (For Patricia, Spanish was her first language, and she learned English when she entered school at the age of five.)

"I can recall," laughs Patricia, "that sometimes the ladies wouldn't have a payment and would send one of the children to the door when we knocked. The child would say, 'My mom says she's not here.' We would have to move on to the next stop; but we would be sure to collect double on the next trip."

Patricia discovered the world of commerce was fun, exciting and the only way of life she knew. She learned marketing (giving the people what they want at a fair price), the importance of the contract (she's a legal eagle when it comes to reading, correcting, and negotiating contracts) and payment (it's no good to sell something if you can't collect the payment). These lessons have served her well with her businesses.

Patricia went to college in New Mexico, graduated and went to work as a Territory Sales Manager for a Fortune 50 company. She decided there had to be more to life; she had developed enough marketing skills to start her own marketing consultant business. So, she did. She made another change when she sold the business a few years later and went "all in" back to get her master's degree. She then had an opportunity to move to D.C., where she identified market ready minority firms and facilitated their introduction to overseas opportunities at the U.S. Commerce Department. In that role, she worked extensively with small businesses and federal agencies on contracting services for the government.

Her "family business" is now larger than life and derived from the lessons Manuela taught.

Education Is Important

Education was an important key for Manuela's children to do economically better than she had in life. Higher education created a foundation and stepping stone to unlimited opportunities. Manuela left school after the third grade to help run a cattle ranch and work on it. She never finished her formal education; but she was continually learning in all aspects of her life. She raised six children and absorbed lessons as they learned in school. She passed the love of learning on to all her children.

Patricia's thirst for knowledge did not cease after school. She continues to acquire factoids and tidbits each day with her son Marcus and encourages him in every way to read books, study and even go to the library. She recently enrolled in a Harvard Business Class for executives and is matriculating through this online and in classroom, year-long learning. When you talk to her about it, she is as excited as if this were her first day of school. She's ready to tell you all about it, how much she's learning and about the amazing people she's met. She never stops learning!

We once joked about her making Marcus go to the library to research and write a report. Here's how it all occurred. The family was going on a trip to Pennsylvania over the summer. Patricia told Marcus he had to research and write a report telling her what there was to see and do in the state using only the nearby public library. I asked Patricia. "In this day and age, who needs to go to the library? Everything you could possibly want to research can be found by going online." She, however, insisted Marcus understand the library system, enjoy the research and experience the feel and smell of the books in that environment. Marcus developed a fact-filled report the family used to visit interesting sites in Pennsylvania.

She has insured that her son is also bi-lingual and proud of his Hispanic heritage. He can converse with his grandmother in her native language. That is certainly a joy for both!

Turned Upside Down

When Manuela was diagnosed with breast cancer a few years back, Patricia and her family attacked the experience just like it was another learning opportunity for the family. They rallied their brothers and their dad. They read up on all the possibilities and treatments. They made sure their mom, her doctors and the family were enlisted to make the experience the best it could be for their mom.

A few years later, Patricia experienced her own health challenge with an aggressive form of leukemia. Patricia attacked the experience just like she would anything else. She, again, learned all about it, the various treatments and prognosis. After spending nine months in the hospital and enduring a bone marrow transplant (her youngest brother was an 100% match), she went into remission. She says, "It's experiences like these that help you set your priorities and determine what is really important in your life." We would agree, as would Manuela. Both Patricia and her mother continue to live life to its fullest and continue learning what life has in store for them.

Education is more than what you absorb in school to obtain that piece of paper. It is a continual process that keeps minds alert, inquisitive and challenged. Manuela totally agrees!!

The author's Grandma, Essie Mae Wilson Holt on the steps of the church after recognition of the author's graduation class from high school. Author is shown in glasses behind her grandmother.

NEVER TOO LATE TO LEARN

You are never too old to set another goal or to dream a new dream.

-- *C.S. Lewis*

My grandma also never stopped learning or encouraging us to learn. When I was about seven or eight years old, I wanted to learn to swim. My mom had had a bad experience and almost drowned when she was young; she was deathly afraid of water. Someone had thrown her into the water, and she went under a couple of times before she was rescued.

My grandma, on the other hand, thought it was important for me to learn to swim. She got a membership to the YWCA one summer, and she and I took lessons together. She didn't know how to swim either and thought it would be a fun experience for both of us. Once a week, we would load up our swimsuits and swimming caps (yes, you wore them back then to keep your hair nice and dry). We would head down to the YWCA and enjoy our lessons. The class consisted of older ladies like my grandmother in one part of the pool and younger children like me on the other end. While I was learning to float, crawl stroke and backstroke, Grandma was learning to tread water and dog paddle. She was so excited at the end of summer when she could stay afloat. I was excited that I could go *cleaaaaaaaaar* across the pool by myself without any flotation devices. It was an exhilarating summer. I learned how much I like being in the water and how relaxing a good swim could be. Grandma became my hero that summer. Who would have thought someone that old would ever learn to swim?

It is never too late to learn something new from someone else, and Grandma proved that to me that summer.

She taught me what's important, and what isn't. And I've never forgotten. And that's what mothers do...

— Steven Herrick, A Place Like This

PART 4 - Cheese and Grits

There may be times when we are powerless to prevent injustice, but there must never be a time when we fail to protest."

--Elie Wiesel

P*eople who serve others with their life's work are special.* **Cheese and Grits** *is one of those grits dishes that make us feel good, comfortable and cheerful even if we are not a true grits fan. But people that can make you feel comfortable while tackling the banner of injustice are a special breed unto themselves. These mothers instilled something in their daughters that said the world is not all about money and position. It is about what you do each day to make it better for others. Service and belief in a cause bigger than what you can see drives these women. Shirley Chisholm once said, "Service is the rent that you pay for room on this earth." I'd say these women and the mothers that raised them should be living in penthouses!*

Rohena Miller

DON'T JUDGE A BOOK BY ITS COVER

My mother had handed down respect for the possibilities...and the will to grasp them.
--Alice Walker

"**W**hat are you?" I inquired. "I'm blaaaa...ck!" she shot back. And, thus began a friendship with an improbable looking black woman who was probably blacker than this little country black Kansas girl raised in the land of Oz.

Rohena (pronounced ro- ee - nah) Miller looks nothing like a black woman. She is as white as any white woman you will see. She has straight, thick auburn hair, angular features and a figure-type found in many white women – large bust and slim hips. But, don't be fooled by her appearance. When she opens her mouth, that southern Louisville, Kentucky drawl and Southern hospitality take control. Her language can be angelic, tactful and corporate-speak one minute; and targeted, direct and colorful the next.

"We lived in the hood," Rohena explains. "My brother and I looked as white as could be. If you didn't learn to defend yourself, you would be beat up every day."

No doubt it was that ferocious tenacity which made Rohena the success she is today. She is the owner of Niche Marketing, a public relations and event production firm. She established one of the greatest events for people of color in the country -- The Grand Gala or Kentucky-Derby-Meets-People-of-Color!" The star-studded Grand Gala included attendance by numerous celebrities--Michael Jordan, Gabriel Union, Regina King, Tyrese Gibson, Jerome Bettis, John Sally, the late Teena Marie and more. Corporate representatives and minority business owners vied to be invited. You were treated like royalty and the privileged for an entire weekend. You'd be picked up at the hotel, transported to the Churchill Downs, exiting to a red carpet complete with security and paparazzi. You were then escorted directly to one of the best suites Churchill Downs offered. (One year, we were next door to the owner of the Houston Texans football team. He had a horse in the race. We talked with him and the people in his suite, rooted for his horse from the balcony and were sad when his horse neither won, shown or placed.) However, like most of

Rohena's projects, the Grand Gala was not without purpose. The Grand Gala linked minority business owners with Corporate America representatives to instill networking and training around growth, development and business opportunities. Rohena ties everything she does to creating business-to-business connections and philanthropic giving. She understands business is about people knowing other people.

Rohena is comfortable in the presence of the rich and famous, as well as top level corporate representatives. They love her for all that she does. Niche Marketing has represented the Field Generals: the African-American Quarterback Club, USA Track and Field, Ryder Cup and the African-Americans associated with the National Basketball Association (NBA). She worked with the Billion Dollar Round Table and its many corporate representatives. She continues to provide support to several corporations about their supplier diversity programs. In addition, she works with minority business owners to help further their career goals, as well as assists with their charitable foundations.

Where did she get the genes that produced fearlessness in the face of challenges? Giving back even when others do not follow her example? Making connections between people without asking anything in return? Let's meet her mom!

Never Be Afraid

Ann Elizabeth Daniels Miller

Ann Elizabeth Daniels Miller was a housewife up until Rohena was 16. She divorced and went back to school to obtain her college degree. Ann held a position with the Airport Authority for 20 years before retiring. Ann did more than work and raise her two children. She was an activist defending civil rights and renouncing social injustices that occurred in Louisville. She obviously ignored the perception and direction of others. After all, she was a black woman who lived in the hood and had two kids that looked white. She never blinked if someone ridiculed or criticized her choices. She taught her daughter to never back down or be afraid of who she was. "If you stand for nothing," Ann would say, "you will fall for anything...period!"

"I have seen her stop in the middle of the street and break up a fight," says Rohena. "I have seen her stand up for one injustice after the other in Louisville and never get deterred. She was instrumental in securing Kentucky's first black priest – a move that didn't sit well with the lily-white Catholic community. She believed in GOD ALWAYS and her will to do right for her family and the community in which we lived. She taught me to never to be afraid to stand up for my beliefs."

The Miller house was by no means a haven. Ann's stubbornness, faith and proclivity for causes did not always sit well with her neighbors or the Louisville community. The house was broken into on numerous occasions; the car was stolen several times. On one occasion, Rohena recalls, "Our garage window was broken. Someone had gone into the house through the window. My Mom knew someone was in the house and ran into it anyway, scaring away the thief. She believed God would protect her and He always did."

Rohena recalls how as a black child who looked white, she had to be prepared every day to defend herself. She attended a private school but had to come home to the hood. She learned to hold her own in both worlds, which is probably why she does the same in the world of business and philanthropy.

Be Respectful of Others

Ann also taught Rohena another valuable lesson that has defined how Rohena conducts her business. It is probably the reason she can move so easily among the world of celebrities, business owners and everyday people. Ann believed strongly in respecting everyone. It did not matter their class in life or their circumstances. You must love and respect everyone.

Rohena began doing volunteer work in the community at a very young age. She used to teach tennis lessons and coach basketball for the neighborhood youth. Even today, she continues to work to uplift others. Each year the National Minority Supplier Development Council (NMSDC) holds a National Conference. In 2005, the year Katrina hit New Orleans, the NMSDC conference was scheduled to be held in New Orleans the following year.

Rohena developed a Day of Caring. She thought it could make a statement for the minority business owners attending the conference to come in early and give back to the community. She and I and her team at Niche Marketing worked to recruit volunteers, seek corporate support for snacks, drinks, paint, brushes etc. She found appropriate activities for the team to perform on Saturday in the community. One team planted trees and flowers in the 9th Ward – one of the hardest hit areas in New Orleans. The other team went to one of the historic African-American districts and painted the outside of an elderly woman's home. The event was a huge success and rewarding to all who participated. We demonstrated the power of minority business owners to make things better for the next generation when we remember where we came from.

For several years thereafter, Day of Caring continued to help enrich communities wherever the NMSDC National Conference was held. Minority business owners, led by Rohena, participated in community activities to help uplift the community – if only for a day. One year, we painted houses in Little Haiti in Miami. We had a mentoring day with children ages 8-18 in Atlanta. Participants in the mentoring experience included both entrepreneurs and corporate executives who enlightened the youngsters on the possibilities for their lives provided they stayed in school and concentrated on their achievements, not their circumstances. As a participant, I know the mentors got as much out of the experience as the children we mentored.

Don't Let Your Circumstances Block Your View of the Possibilities

Ann wasn't afraid when money and financial matters weren't favorable either. She made sure her children always had what they needed and a LITTLE of what they wanted. She went without to make sure her children had braces and attended private schools. She taught Rohena to read at an early age. In sixth grade, Rohena tested for Freshman English and Senior math. Her mom's belief in education and her commitment to providing her children the best education possible resulted in Rohena graduating from high school at age sixteen.

"I can remember one summer my mom saved and saved," recalls Rohena. "She ended up taking her savings, driving my brother and me ten miles over the bridge to New Albany, Indiana to spend the night at a hotel. We swam in the pool, went to the theater and ate great meals. It was a grand vacation and the one I most remember."

Perhaps, this is why Niche Marketing and Rohena have done so much over the years with what seems like so little. She has delivered extraordinary events, found appropriate sponsorships, included key celebrities … all operating on slim budgets.

Rohena's most recent creation is all about her heart and her true purpose. She married a wonderful gentleman, Farad Ali, who had children. She became an instant mother and jumped right in to instill in her children her view of the possibilities in the world. It was partly the youngest of the new family that became her encouragement to create a new world – Planet Mogul. She has worked on it for over five years and in 2017, it has come to fruition. Planet Mogul is an amazing digital platform designed to teach entrepreneurship worldwide to current and wannabe young entrepreneurs. Her latest release includes educational tools, kid-friendly components for children as young as four, a cartoon and industry academy resources. The offering helps global corporations and educators understand how to develop the entrepreneurs of the future, while explaining industry, supply chains and business connections. The focus is creating a more diverse segment of suppliers, both ethnically and globally. (Visit www.planetmogul.com.)

Planet Mogul is more than a game, it is Rohena's vision and tenacity to create the world we all want to see—diverse, talented, enriched, confident entrepreneurs around the globe. As with all her projects, Planet Mogul was created by diverse suppliers and young people. The cartoon was developed by a group of young people associated with the Young Entrepreneurs Project (YEP).

It is also the reason that when you talk to Rohena, you understand her vision to do great things in the world for people and to impact the circumstances of others. Her favorite saying is "create the world you want to see." She has certainly taken that to heart. Whether we are talking Planet Mogul, Day of Caring or a myriad of other causes, Rohena is always ready to step up to make the occasions and the outcome work. It doesn't matter how big the dream or how difficult it may seem, Rohena is never afraid and understands you can overcome your circumstances. It is her passion to instill that belief in others that keeps her motivated!

Margo J. Posey

ADVOCATE. WARRIOR. SERVANT.

Life is not important except in the impact it has on other lives.
--Jackie Robinson

There are special people in this world that God puts in place to be a direct blessing to others. Mothers are one of those blessed creatures. But, once in a great while a mother and a leader are melded together to create what I call a "servant warrior." This warrior serves others relentlessly; advocates justice for all; and expects little or nothing in return. They don't even realize they are a warrior. This is who they are; it is their DNA; and they wouldn't know how to be anything else. As a benefactor of the mentorship, leadership and friendship of these personages, I say thank

138

you! This chapter is about one of my favorite servant warriors.

If you saw her on the street or in a meeting, you would think how striking she is. I tease her about being a "diva on a budget." Blond-grey hair, pistachio green eyes, a smile or a frown depending upon her disposition. (Her face tells you just what she's thinking). The requisite pearls encircle her neck because that is what divas of a certain generation or upbringing wear. She is outfitted in a fashionable dress. (She almost never wears jeans, except trendy jeans when she's ready to let her hair down.) She is one-of-a-kind, Margo J. Posey.

Margo is the President of the Dallas/Fort Worth Minority Supplier Development Council, the organization that has connected me to many of the women in this book. She is a leader who has brought together countless minority owned businesses and corporate/public sector buyers in North Texas to create real business engagement. While she might not consider herself a warrior, the hundreds of minority-owned businesses she represents would boldly disagree. She is one of our biggest champions and advocates. She continues to inch minority business inclusion progress forward. And the servant warrior that she is would never take credit for any of it.

I met Margo as a part of her organization. We took a cautious approach to each other when we first met. She wasn't sure "where I was coming from" and didn't know where I had been. I came to volunteer and felt no need to explain myself. Why did it matter? The funny thing was, both of us were too polite and tactful to verbalize our doubts. Instead, we warily observed each other maneuver around the Council. We began to develop a healthy working relationship consisting of respect and support. Inevitably, the relationship morphed into a friendship. The passion I have for minority business inclusion was ignited by embers planted by Margo. I learned what a diverse supplier was, why there was a need to treat them "differently" and how far we have yet to go to make minority inclusion in the supply chain a true reality. I also learned what being certified as a diverse supplier meant and the persistence it required to build business relationships while tagged as a "minority."

As I began to write this book, I knew Margo and her mother had to appear somewhere in it. It took some convincing. She, after all, is a servant warrior – doing rather than talking about it. However, I knew her impact on my life and was curious about how she came to be. Part of the story had to be told. What lessons did her mother pass along that created this servant warrior? It is a "be strong – willingness to keep going" and a caring, listening attitude toward all stations of life.

<u>A Willingness to Keep Going</u>

In a world and generation of black and white, Lois Jean Bailey was a survivor. She may not have been perceived as black enough or white enough or smart enough or elegant enough, but she was certainly strong enough. As any survivor will tell you, you must be focused on the outcome, sometimes tread alone and be your own cheerleader when others fade away. It is not a simple task and it becomes even more difficult when you are a black woman in America.

Lois learned this early in life. She was beautiful, but

maybe not quite beautiful enough. Her sister and her mother outshined her. Things she wanted out of life she had to work hard to obtain. There were no easy roads or a benefactor waiting to shower her with gifts. Everything she had, she earned. It required dedication, commitment and focus.

Four Generations left to right, Grandmother Lillie Reynolds, Margo J. Posey holding daughter Mercedes and mother Lois Jean Bailey (standing)

"One of the things I admire most about my mom," recalls Margo, "is no matter what was going on in her life, she still was willing to get up every morning and keep going."

Lois left high school early but returned to complete her diploma and obtain further education. She thought nursing school might be her destiny but opted for accounting instead. It served her well. For over twenty years she served as a bookkeeper to the United Auto Workers in Akron, Ohio.

Lois raised three children – two girls and a boy. It wasn't always easy. She was a strict disciplinarian, especially with her eldest child, Margo.

"I always felt and knew I was loved," remembers Margo, "even when I was in trouble for something. She would be angriest when you didn't tell her the truth. In my mom's world there was no reason to lie."

Margo tells the story of sneaking out of the house with her mom's watch without permission. She wore the watch one afternoon around the neighborhood, showing it to all her friends. When she returned home, she replaced it in its spot – her mom none the wiser. Or so she thought. Like all moms with eyes in the back of their head, Lois suspected that someone had been playing with her things and immediately questioned Margo about it. Margo denied it. Her mom proceeded to march Margo over to the neighbors and ask the children if they had ever seen the watch before. "You mean Margo's watch?" they replied. Needless to say, it did not end well for Margo. But she learned that non-truths can have severe consequences, so you might as well tell the truth.

Getting up each morning for Lois meant pursuing her dreams and achieving her goals. She wanted to raise her children in a home of their own. It wasn't a time when women could just go out and buy a house on their own. That didn't deter Lois. She saved for her house. When the time and money were right, she was able to secure a mortgage (a major feat in itself) and raised her three children in it.

"I can recall when I was graduating from high school," says Margo, "I had the opportunity to go to Smith College. It would have, however, required my mom to sign for a loan using the house as collateral. She wouldn't do it. She had worked hard to buy the house and wouldn't let me or anyone else have the opportunity to take it from her. At the time I was disappointed, but today I understand how precious that achievement was to my mother."

Much like her mother, Margo also developed a "work hard for what you want" attitude. Her early childhood dreams included becoming a wife and mother. It was the era of "Leave It to Beaver" and June Cleaver seemed to live a charmed life. Margo won a modeling contest with one of the local department stores and her dreams switched to be a model or an actress. But just like her mother, hard work found her early. The contest led to a job with the local department store. She began working at sixteen and hasn't stopped since.

Today, as a champion for minority business inclusion, her days are filled with connecting corporate and public sector buyers with minority owned businesses. She starts her day with breakfast meetings, continues with events/sessions throughout the day and often ends the day attending a reception or dinner function. Changing how people build business relationships and how they do business is not easy. Margo has gained the respect of business people in North Texas and nationwide with her honesty and support.

And about that acting dream, the "ham" is still buried within her and not very deeply I might add. Attend her organization's famed Oscar-like "E Awards" banquet and you'll see a bit of it shine through.

A Listening Ear

Lois was not just about herself and her family. She also cared about her neighbors and fellow workers. It was not unusual for her to be found at home, extending a listening ear. She did not need to dispense advice or suggestions. She simply provided a priestly ear for those going through tough times in life. Occasionally, she took her generosity a step further.

One time, Margo had a young friend who became pregnant and her parents kicked her out of the house. Margo brought the friend home to stay for a couple of nights until plans could be made for where she could go. When Margo explained to Lois the situation, Lois immediately proceeded to make up Margo's bed for the guest. She told Margo to just sleep on the couch. For the duration of the pregnancy the friend lived with them – in Margo's room! Lois waited on the young girl, treated her like royalty and dared Margo to complain.

"I couldn't believe it," exclaims Margo. "My mom was a stickler for being on time. Nothing would make her late for work. However, when my friend moved in, my mom would wait on her to get ready and then drop her off, even if it delayed her own schedule a few minutes. When I would ask my mom about the special treatment, she would just reply that my friend needed help and she was willing to provide it."

Lois had a big heart and she spread her generosity and caring on others. It was a key lesson Margo learned growing up. Visit Margo's offices today and you will find her sitting down listening to a business owner harangue about the lack of commitment by Corporate America to minority business or visiting on the phone with a corporate member befuddled about finding large, capable minority owned businesses to fill their supply chain pipeline. She listens. She doesn't control the bottom-line or the business decisions of any of these companies (big or small), but she does have an impact. She engages, asks questions, and sometimes even makes suggestions.

She is also involved in her "spare time" with causes impacting the community. She may be delivering a home-cooked meal to someone sick or supporting a cause that helps young "chaps" prepare for the world.

"Without the sense of caring, there can be no sense of community," quotes Anthony D'Angelo. Margo has both a sense of caring and a sense of community. She is a servant warrior. If confronted with her deeds, she is humble and self-effacing. She would never admit she makes any difference. We – her mentees and friends -- would adamantly beg to differ.

Alma Garcia

SOULFUL SISTER -- HERMANA CON ALMA

*Beautiful young people
are accidents of nature,
but beautiful old people are works of art.*

--Eleanor Roosevelt

One look and you know she is not the traditional "soul sister" of urban lexicology. Instead, you face two big brown eyes crowned with long lush lashes (all real by the way), a fashionably cropped "do," upon a lithe, fit body accustomed to walking, biking and hiking. You are in the presence of one Alma Garcia, (Spanish for "soul"). Her given name fits her to a T. She is holistic, vegetarian, spiritual and *soulful.*

147

Her world demands respect for her Mexican heritage, yet she thrives on life's variety and possibilities. It is that acceptance of the mosaic of life that still beckons her through her work, play and friends. Sometimes testy and always inquisitive, Alma is neither boring nor bored.

I am not sure exactly how we first met. It might have been at an event with the Women's Business Council – Southwest in Dallas. She was once employed as the Events Director for the organization and I have had the joy of working with her on several of the Council's event committees. We also could have first met through mutual friends. However we met, we have become friends and she is indeed a "soulful sister."

Alma's day job now focuses on the elderly and those in need of home care support. It seems a fitting match for one so giving and spiritual. Alma's philanthropic commitments have included being the volunteer Executive Director of Dream Angels, Inc., an organization dedicated to expanding the horizons for young women through various educational, cultural and business experiences. And, in the true fashion of expanding her reach and impact, she leads global studies programs in Peru and Cuba through Bright Light Volunteers.

Her willingness to face the challenges and opportunities of life are directly related to the woman who raised her. Her commitment to family can be attributed to her mother, as well. Life throws a lot of curve balls at you, but you must be able to catch, assess and move on.

A Fierce Determination

Juanita Pesina (aka "vieja" or wife/old woman in Spanish) was raised in Victoria, Texas. Her mother died

Alma Garcia's mother, Juanita Pesina

when she was just seven, leaving the young girl to be a surrogate caretaker to her three younger brothers and her father. It was a daunting task for one so young. Her formal education ended in elementary school, as she became responsible for keeping a clean home, putting food on the table and making sure the men in the house had clean, ironed clothes to wear. Juanita had no women around as role models, but she managed to do what had to be done. Her father was a carpenter who worked hard to provide for his family. Juanita's one outlet was her paternal uncle who had a Model T car and liked to work on cars. Juanita would occasionally enjoy watching him work on vehicles when she had a moment to get away from chores.

"My mom didn't have normal childhood experiences like other girls," remarks Alma. "There were no dolls, tea sets, frilly dresses or birthday parties. She was too busy cleaning, cooking and ironing to have fun."

Juanita married and had her first child around 18 or 19. The family lived with her mother-in-law in Mexico. Her husband decided to seek better opportunities by going to the United States. He promised to send for them when he got settled. Meanwhile, Juanita remained with her mother-in-law.

At some point, Juanita grew tired of waiting for word from her husband to follow him to the States. Life couldn't have been easy with the mother-in-law, her son and no husband around. She decided to pack up and head to the U.S. on her own. Though her mother-in-law protested and warned her of the dangers, Juanita was determined to unite her little family. With minimal money and unsure exactly where her husband was, she took her son and headed to west Texas. She couldn't swim but crossed the Rio Grande. She hitchhiked from place to place. Once, a guy in a truck picked them up. Juanita was okay at first but began to feel uncomfortable about the situation. She jumped from the vehicle with her son in her arms and continued to walk to where she thought her husband might be.

Juanita only spoke Spanish – no English. She went from town to town describing her husband. Eventually, she ended up at a diner in a little Texas town. The patrons told her there was a guy staying at the Bracero's boarding house that fit the description. She walked to the boarding house and walked right up on him! He was surprised; but Juanita was determined to make an honest man out of him!

Eventually the family left west Texas and moved to the Dallas/Fort Worth area. They had six children total. Juanita was a hardworking and loving mother. She worked two jobs while Alma was growing up. Juanita arose at 4:00 am to pack her husband's lunchbox with fresh tortillas, caldo de res (Mexican beef soup), arroz (rice) and frijoles (beans) before reporting to work, herself, at 7:00 a.m. in the cafeteria at Kraft's manufacturing plant in Garland, Texas. She would then go to her second job at a local nursing home and not return home until 11:00 p.m.

Juanita's experiences growing up made her an extremely devoted mother to her own six children. She did all she knew how to do to make her children's lives and experiences wonderful.

"I never appreciated my mother's commitment to both her job and her family until I became an adult," praises Alma. "Looking back, I realize she always worked hard and never complained."

Juanita, who had never had a birthday party, was rewarded by her children with her first birthday party at age 84. She was the star of the party. One of the gifts was a tea set! The rewards of a fierce determination and uncompromising love were on display that day. More importantly, the children said THANK YOU to a loving, caring mother!

Alma also took a circuitous journey to arrive where she is today. Born in Abernathy, Texas, she graduated from the Garland, Texas public school system after her family moved to the Dallas area. Her early interest was in becoming a missionary. The path could not only provide interaction with a variety of people, but also allow her to help others. She also had a love of rocks and music.

"To this day, rocks still fascinate me, and I am always searching for odd-shaped rocks when hiking," says Alma. "I thought I would grow up to be a geologist or play in an orchestra. I still listen to Mahler, Rachmaninoff and other great composers. They feed my soul and keep me connected to symphonic music."

As fate would have it, however, Alma's early career path did not entirely match up with her youthful interest. Instead, she started her career as a fund development manager for a non-profit in New Mexico. It allowed her to interact with a diverse group of people, intermingle with donors and patrons and fan her passion for helping others. She has traveled the country, met fascinating people and soaked in the variety of cultures and people. She spent time in Washington, DC and New Mexico before settling back in the Dallas/Fort Worth area to raise her son, Cuatro, and adopted daughter, Julienne.

The return to Dallas allowed Alma to reunite with her aging mom and the rest of her family. She realizes that not only is motherhood the most important job on the planet, but also that much of what she learned about it, she learned from her own mother.

Alma takes motherhood and the commitment it involves seriously. All you must do is meet her son, Cuatro, and you know how well she has succeeded. When Cuatro decided he was going to be a vegetarian, Alma joined him in his endeavor. Together, she and Cuatro often enjoy various cultural events throughout the Dallas area. They hike, bike and Alma enjoys watching Cuatro perform on his skateboard. Her home is filled with music but NO television.

She has also included Cuatro in her volunteer efforts to assist those in need. Alma is a demanding mom who wants her son to understand the consequences of his actions and inactions. She has her commitment right. If the choice is between visiting with friends and participating with her son, Cuatro wins out every time.

Disarm Through Kindness

If you're having trouble with a client, a boss, a sibling, a spouse, Juanita has some advice for you. "Disarm your enemies by being kind to them."

Juanita loved the church. Her husband was not as spiritual at first. Juanita did not drive, but she wanted to go to church, so she would walk for hours to the little church she attended in west Texas. She never complained about the walk or about her husband. She would not let anyone sabotage her faith. She just got up and went. Eventually, she learned to drive.

When Alma went through her divorce, Juanita coached her through it and encouraged Alma not to say any disparaging words about her ex-husband and Cuatro's father. Alma took the advice and allowed Cuatro to make his own decisions about the relationship.

In some of her work positions, it was not always the easiest life to be the only woman of color in the workplace. There are many in this book who could and would attest to that. Cultural differences, social ignorance and a spirit of envy can often raise its ugly head when it should be about getting the job done.

Juanita had several occasions on her jobs when people were not respectful to her, but she always responded with kindness. "My mom shared times with me," reflects Alma, "when she encountered difficult people. She would disarm them with her kindness. Amazingly, the situations often came from the women you would least expect – church ladies!"

Alma, too, has encountered people who wished her to stumble because she didn't look like them, act like them or want to be like them.

"I carried on," affirms Alma. "I sprinkled little acts of kindness throughout my journey. It has become my personal mantra. It works! They don't know what hit them!"

Alma tells the story of a Hispanic cleaning lady who found Alma working quite late at the office. The cleaning lady was so proud to see a successful Hispanic woman with her own office. Alma felt empowered by the conversation with the lady. All the hard work and challenges facing her seemed to dissipate just with a short conversation with this wonderful cleaning lady. This act of kindness by the cleaning lady has kept Alma vigilant through various challenges and obstacles.

Relationships Take Time

We have all had times when we thought our mothers had no idea what they were talking about. They cautioned us on everything, and sometimes we listened and sometimes we did not. It is not unusual for there to be a period when mother and daughter don't see eye-to-eye. Juanita and Alma had such a period in their lives.

But there were some special moments that bonded them even closer together. One was when Alma was in Santa Fe and had a miscarriage. Juanita comforted and consoled Alma by sharing her own personal experience of a miscarriage. Alma had no idea that Juanita had faced such a situation.

After Alma's father died, Juanita decided to spend time with Alma and Cuatro in New Mexico. It was during that time Alma committed herself to building back a stronger relationship with her mom. Juanita stayed for two months and enjoyed her time with Alma and Cuatro. Since Alma moved back to the Dallas area, the relationship has grown even stronger.

"I keep a guest book in my home for visitors to write in when they visit," says Alma. "One day, while I was at work, my mother decided to provide an entry in the book. I couldn't believe it. It was wonderful and such a blessing."

Juanita is 91 years young and challenged with dementia. This requires her children to be vigilant caregivers. Alma and her sister provide weekend care for Juanita at her home. The family is stronger and tighter than ever. Juanita passed her lessons and blessings to the next generation. Her faith in God, her "never defeated attitude" and her love of her children and family are all lessons Alma treasures and follows.

PART 5 - Build Your Own Grits

A mother's love liberates.

--Maya Angelou

S*ometimes in life you meet that one person who reminds you that it alright to go your own way and do your own thing. The problem is most of us have forgotten those dreams or are simply too confined by the issues of stability and the next thing in our life to hear the whispers.* **Build Your Own Grits** *contains the story of just one woman and her mother who had the foresight to recognize the talent and creativity of her daughter – who was nothing like her – and encourage the dreams. Being an artist (music, painter, dancer, writer...) can be a very nontraditional and hard life. However, what they bring to you and me to enjoy is the glory and passion that is in our hearts trying to escape the day-to-day struggles of our existence. Artist,* **Build Your Own!** *We love you for it!*

Viola Delgado in her favorite overalls.
Photo by Leticia Alaniz © 2016

THE ARTIST

If you have a mom,
there is nowhere you are likely to go
where a prayer has not already been.
--Robert Brault

In today's world the term "artist" has been associated with all means of expression including music, film, writing, rappin' and more. This creative bent is interpretive, imaginative and often visual. In the old-fashioned

159

explanation, Webster defines "artist" as a person who practices one of the fine arts, especially a painter or sculptor.

Viola Delgado, "The Artist," fits the mold of the latter. She is creative and imaginative. She delivers a kaleidoscope of visual experiences. She is a free spirit. Viola is a mane of thick grey hair, "Erkle" style black rimmed glasses, paint-splattered overalls draped with an accent scarf around her neck, and you can usually find her in a bevy of laughing, smiling *compadres*. Organization, selling, managing are not her strengths. Have a cup of coffee with her. Keep a pen and napkin handy and you will soon see some amazing art doodles. Her hands are in motion explaining the next exciting creative art project she is developing for a group of grade school children. Or, she's describing how she and a young autistic boy are creating the art found within him. Or, watch the storyteller emerge as she demonstrates another period of misadventure intersecting her life. When she is finally still and reflective, you can feel the breadth and depth of her spirit; visualize it in her series on clouds; behold a mosaic come to life, flower unfold or cloud drift away. Her art is her passion and her passion is her art! My first interaction with Viola (or "V" as I often call her) came about by way of an introduction through a mutual friend. We immediately clicked. Born in the same month, near the same age, and tied to creativity as a way of life, we found something in common from the start. She is the free spirit I wish I were. Viola is "all in" on her art and curating art. Leaving behind job stability, she devotes her life and her time to her art. Occasionally, you see the more thoughtful, pensive, self-deprecating side of her. Her friends are her friends always. Her family is her family always. And she would do anything that she could for each of them.

What is amazing about Viola is the mother who let her be who she is despite the concern for Viola's overall welfare. Viola learned many lessons from this amazing woman and perhaps the greatest was to be true to oneself.

Jesusa Rodriguez Delgado,
mother of Viola Delgado

Nurturing Your Opposite

It's hard to believe how different Viola is from her mother – or at least to hear her tell you. One is tall and lean; the other short and not so lean. One is organized and businesslike; the other less so. One crunches numbers and plans each step; the other, not so much. Both, however, are lovers of people and would help anyone, any time. Jesusa Rodriguez Delgado was born in Sinton, Texas. When she was young, she worked with her grandfather and kept the books. She managed the payroll and accounts for

161

migrant workers that her grandfather hired to work in the fields. She was a bit of a tomboy, but she also knew how to act and dress like a lady. She enjoyed working alongside her father who was always fixing some piece of machinery. She would hand him the tools and watch him as he repaired stuff. When she wasn't working alongside her dad or grandfather, you could find Jesusa on the playing field. She loved to play fast-pitch baseball (no slow softball for her). She was a top player and enjoyed playing even after she married.

Jesusa worked at one thing or another growing up. She seemed to always find something to do. She worked for a couple who owned a clothing store. She was hired to watch their child; however, because of her height, she would model the store dresses for the ladies. They would often buy based upon how well the dress looked on Jesusa. She never got any of the clothes, but she did have the opportunity to ride the train to Dallas a couple of times while the couple shopped for items for their store.

Jesusa didn't marry until she was 21 (old by her cultural standards). After marriage, she continued to work. New doctors in town needed someone who was bilingual to help them in their clinic. She would translate the problem and convey to the patients the recommended remedy. The doctors found Jesusa engaging and competent in her role. They decided to train her to be their nurse. She remained with them for a time. When she became pregnant, the doctors gave Jesusa plenty of vitamins and pre-natal care.

Viola made her proud entrance into the world in Sinton, Texas weighing over nine pounds! ("It was all those damn vitamins," laughs Viola.) Four more children would follow Viola, including another daughter arriving eight years after Viola's birth.

Jesusa doted on her children and made them the most important part of her world. She stayed home to raise them. She would take on occasional little jobs but would make sure it was when the children were at school. She was involved in every aspect of her children's lives. She was everywhere doing everything.

Her husband made sure Jesusa always had a car in case of an emergency with the children. She decided to put the car to use while the children were at school. She began driving women in the neighborhood to work at the Plymouth Oil compound where all the workers and executives lived. On occasion, Jesusa would also clean houses. One of the executive houses that she cleaned would one day become the home of the Delgados. It went on the market and Jesusa and her husband decided to buy the house.

Jesusa strove to make sure her children lived a good life. To entertain them, she would often draw stick pictures on paper sacks for them to color. Viola was about four or five. It was in those moments Viola found the world of art. She discovered the possibilities and an imaginary world of the exploits by her mom's stick figures. It became clear to Jesusa that her eldest daughter would not be like her – bookkeeper, nurse, business person, etc. Instead, Viola seemed happiest when left to her own imaginative, creative world of art. Jesusa encouraged her daughter each day to be the best she could be at what she loved to do.

Action-Oriented Love

Jesusa's caring didn't stop with her family. She loved to visit and help people. No one was any better or worse than anyone else in Jesusa's eyes. We were all God's children and she wanted her children to understand that. Jesusa had an answer for each situation. When one of her nephews wasn't eating properly at school, she decided to work in the school cafeteria to make sure that he would eat the right things every day.

Jesusa was also very political and would take people to the polls, so they could vote. She was involved with the Democratic Party and worked with many of the politicians to get them elected.

"My mother never pushed me to get married, buy a house, and have kids," recalls Viola. "She used to tell me 'Friendships are more important than a man.' She encouraged me to have plenty of friends and never pressured me to 'settle down.'"

Thus, Viola learned to love and appreciate people by observing her mom. Jesusa didn't hesitate to help others. Throughout her life, she sought to be of assistance to her children and to others.

Viola is much like her. She has a boatload of acquaintances and friends. Each has a Viola story to tell and it usually ends in laughter. She is kind hearted and would give you her last dime if she thought you needed it more than she did. While sometimes people might take advantage of her good heart, she seems to survive and thrive anyway.

At a birthday party for her at a local restaurant, Viola had a host of women ready to eat, laugh and joke with her. One of her friends traveled to Dallas from Colorado and joined in the fun. Laughter, food, drinks, stories and jokes filled the afternoon. I, as one of the "honorary" Latinas often needed a translation or two on some of the giggles but soon caught on and had a fabulous time. It's like that hanging out with Viola. Her friends become your friends. She is invited to many "artsy" events in Dallas and you can be sure she will support her friends while dragging along other friends to network and increase the attendance.

In this respect, Viola is very much like her mom. She is fun, funny and never met a stranger she couldn't help!

Allowing Dreams to Soar

"Turn a penny into a quarter," Jesusa would say to Viola all the time. It was her way of telling Viola it was okay not to follow the crowd. Be yourself and follow your dream.

"I didn't always understand what that meant until I was much older," says Viola. "But I did know she encouraged me in art and my career. She taught me to dream."

Viola taught for a time and then left the school district to advance her art career. She began taking art classes at the local college.

"I was horrible at it at first," states Viola. "Eventually I learned some techniques. I especially liked print making. Coming up with ideas was easy for me and print making made my ideas come to life."

There was an extraordinary art school in Alexandria, VA. One of Viola's friends (Elva Perez) lived and worked in the area and suggested that Viola try to be accepted into the school. Elva offered Viola a place to stay free while she went to school. Viola could concentrate on her art. The print making school only accepted a handful of students each year. You had to send two pieces of your art for evaluation. If the school liked them, you had an opportunity to attend the school. Viola was nervous and anxious but submitted her artwork. She was filled with anxious anticipation. How could she leave her family and move so far away for school? Could she even make it into the school? Was her art passable for admission? All the worries subsided when she was officially accepted. Her art was not only credible; it was good. Viola ended up enrolling, staying with Elva while she went to school and eventually graduating. Then, both returned to Dallas to live.

When Viola held her first exhibit, it was a hit! She had found her direction. She became the curator for the Latino Cultural Center in Dallas. She had a steady job and could still create her art. She eventually left the cultural center and turned full time to her art. Since then, she has completed several public art pieces. One of her glass mosaic medallions can be found on the floor in Terminal D of the DFW International Airport. In 2012, she was the first artist to have a single display of artwork at a Dallas Area Rapid Transit station. Over 52 pieces of her artwork are on display at the Rockwall Station. The art will live on long past Viola. Her free spirit will forever be free to the train and bus riders passing through the station. "My mom used to tell me she had eyes everywhere," says Viola. "When she was sick and in the bed all the time, we talked a lot. She told me how she introduced me to Ms. Cindy, one of my mentors and why. My mom knew she didn't have the know-how to walk me through being an artist. Ms. Cindy could and would make sure I did all right. It was an amazing thing for my mom to release me to someone else; she didn't want to keep me under her wing and stifle my growth."

Viola was living at home when her mom became ill. "I guess I should say that mom died of complications from Parkinson's caused by pesticides," said Viola. "Since they worked the fields all that spray accumulated in her brain stem, causing her illness. She was always careful to wash all her fruits and veggies. She was in a study with a doctor who went on to take this research to the Einstein Institute in New York. She died shortly after he left. They had such a close relationship. But, then, Jesusa was like that with all the people she met.

Jesusa insisted that Viola get an apartment of her own. She didn't want Viola thinking she had to take care of her dad when Jesusa passed away. She felt Viola was too young to take on all that responsibility. Viola had lived in her apartment for over a year when Jesusa finally passed away. Once again, Jesusa was taking care and pushing her eldest daughter to be all that she could be.

Her mom did not live to see the fabulous demonstration of her daughter's talent from stick people to huge public displays. Jesusa, however, knew all along her Viola would make it in the world!

Viola's artwork graces several public places, as well as lives in the hands of singular patrons. When I was almost finished with this book, I reached out to Viola to see if she would do a piece of art to grace the cover of my book. We talked about it over coffee a couple of times. Then one Saturday afternoon as we sat in the sunshine at one of our favorite local tacos stands, Viola suggested we not do a new work but instead use one of her existing pieces. I couldn't believe it. It was one of my favorite pieces by her and she was giving it to me to put on the cover of this book. After further discussion, we both knew this was the only painting that would really capture the spirit of the book. The painting is called *"Mommy Arriving"* It says all that I was trying to say about the amazing spirit of mothers (women) and how that spirit lives on and on and on from generation to generation. *(Thank you, Viola, for capturing in art what I hope I have captured in words!)*

PART 6 - Kiss My Grits

I am a strong woman because a strong woman raised me.

--Unknown

*O*ne of the biggest obstacles I see with women entrepreneurs and business leaders is a hesitancy to tackle something new or great. I am not a mother, but I am a daughter, auntie and great-auntie. If there is one thing I can impart to my nieces that was passed on to me by my mother and grandmother, it is confidence. Why do you worry about your weaknesses? Take the gifts given you by your Creator and use them up! **Kiss My Grits** is about mothers who empowered their daughters early in life to be confident in who they are and what they wanted to do with their lives. It is, perhaps, the greatest gift alongside the love a mother can give her daughter. Don't let anyone tell you that you can't do something. Because you can!

Melinda Marcus

ANALYZE THIS...

Mothers *hold their children's hands for a short while, but their hearts forever.*

--Unknown

When I first met Melinda Marcus, she wore hats and was known as the "Ad Hatter." It was her trademark marketing tool and everyone who knew her could spot her because of the hats with chestnut hair cascading below them. She wore them everywhere – in meetings with CEOs, at events, for lunch, coaching/teaching. Our first encounter was in Leadership Texas, a class designed to introduce women leaders in Texas to some of the issues, culture and history of Texas while bonding and networking with ninety-nine other women leaders from around the state. Melinda is an exceptional storyteller. She finds interesting ways to get your attention and keep it. It is probably why she is also such a sought-after speaker. She hones her craft, believes in practicing regularly and establishes a setting fit for the audience. She is an expert in the art and science of influence. Those skills have served her well as the President and leader of Influence Advisors. Melinda speaks and consults globally on how to leverage proven strategies in Persuasive Psychology, Body Language and Strategic Messaging to win business.

She is not boasting when she says, ""I show executives how to influence decisions before they lose big opportunities. I've helped clients close multi-million-dollar contracts and grow their assets by more than $279 million."

Melinda Marcus and her mother, Dorothy Marcus

Psych

Melinda is the daughter of a psychoanalyst and a clinical social worker. The family dinner table conversation was often about psychology and relationship building. Her mother, Dorothy Marcus (nicknamed Dottie) was a speech therapist initially. When she and her husband decided to move to New Orleans in the early 1950s, Dottie discovered there were no other experts in speech therapy in the city. She recognized an opportunity and started the city's first Speech and Hearing Clinic. After her children were away in college, Dottie decided to go to graduate school and get her master's in social work. She had a wonderful second career counseling people one-on-one.

As a young child, Melinda, wanted to be "Superman" – (not Superwoman, who she viewed at the time as more of a sidekick). "Little girls didn't have superhero role models like they do now," says Melinda. Perhaps that is why initially she wanted to be a psychoanalyst like her dad. "Instead, I discovered I could work with crazy people and have more fun if I went into advertising," laughs Melinda.

The truth is, however, that Melinda stuck closer to the "superhero" role model her mom provided. Melinda didn't stray too far from the fold in that respect. "I was very touched at my mother's funeral when several of her patients came up and introduced themselves to me," reminisces Melinda. "Each had a story about how my mom had helped them, their children and their families."

Melinda savors the opportunity to work one-on-one with people to help them realize their full potential and dreams. She does it by coaching them on how to leverage proven and tested techniques in Persuasive Psychology, Body Language, and Strategic Messaging to influence decisions before they lose big opportunities. You can see her eyes light up when she tells you over lunch how one coaching client thanked her for helping him gain his "swagger," so he could deliver the best presentation of his career and win a big promotion to become President of a global company. Melinda has built Influence Advisors into a successful, one-of-a-kind consulting business by combining the understanding of the Science of Influence with her experience advising top corporate executives and business owners. Melinda consults and speaks internationally and was recognized by National Speakers Association as a CSP (Certified Speaking Professional) - a designation earned by only 12% of speakers globally.

<u>Beating the Bullies</u>

Dottie didn't believe in bullying. She told Melinda, "Bullies are just cowards with louder voices." Per Dottie, when someone is trying to control you through intimidation, insults or humiliation, you must stand up to them immediately. She would tell Melinda, "Do not just take it or give in with the hope that they will magically change and be nicer and more respectful. The only way to stop bad behavior is to take a stand, even if it hurts."

Melinda thought the whole idea was both scary and impossible when she was young. But she has found this lesson to be a proven truth. It was helpful when she was young, and she has confirmed the adage as an adult. You can imagine the "bullying" and humiliation one can encounter in the advertising industry. Can we say, "Mad

Men?" In the competitive world of ad agencies, or even dealing with some clients, one can encounter trials.

"I can always hear my mom's voice urging me to 'stand my ground,'" says Melinda. "Sometimes I didn't want to have a confrontation, so I would just wait it out. That was a BIG mistake because that just prolonged the agony." Melinda found that by taking a stand against a bully, they often backed down and the working relationship improved. She remembered two bullies that became successful referral sources for her.

Joy of Life

Repeatedly, we hear about women who know who they are, stand up for what they believe and are comfortable being who they are. Dottie Marcus was one of those women. She lived true to her values and you always knew where she stood. Even before she became a social worker, she believed in standing up for those who could not stand up for themselves. She was warm, optimistic, and genuine. She made friends easily. Whether it was visiting with her peers or mingling with students her daughter's age, when she went back to school at age 50, Dottie found it fun and exciting to meet new people and develop friendships.

"My mom knew how to have fun," says Melinda. "She loved golf and amazingly shot THREE holes in one! She took up French lessons late in life and we had a great experience traveling to France with her as the family translator. She had what the French call a 'joie de vie' or joy of life!"

Sadly, Dottie passed away in her mid-sixties, but she left a legacy for her daughter and family. Melinda's dad practiced psychoanalysis into his nineties. And, all you must do is go to one of Melinda's seminars and you will have a joyous and fun experience. First, it's the slides. Melinda believes in Macs. It could be because of her advertising background, but I believe it is because she still likes creating with a child's heart. From barking dogs, to exploding doors or giving away millions (you'll have to ask her about that); it will make you laugh, keep you entertained and teach you something that will benefit your life. She also has the "joy of life!"

The author's grandmother, Essie Mae Wilson Holt (on the far left), great grandfather Dee Wilson (center) and great aunts and uncles. Photo was taken of great grandfather surrounded by his nine children at his 89th birthday celebration.

LOSING IS NOT AN OPTION

*We are not interested
in the possibilities of defeat;
they do not exist.*

-- Queen Victoria

I am a competitive animal. I like to win; get disgusted when I lose; and enjoy the competitive nature sports emphasizes. Some may call it arrogant, others passionate and still others cocky. But I have rarely stifled my tongue when I believe I am right or when I am playing a sport. I will hustle (talented or not); I will trash talk (especially when I am winning) and I have been known to lose my temper now and then when an injustice by the referee has not been rectified. Let me be clear – I do not always win – but I certainly try to win. Not at all cost. I do appreciate the rules when applied fairly, whether in sports or business. My adrenaline ratchets up a notch when there is competition involved. I blame this trait on my loving and sweet maternal grandmother and the neighborhood in which I grew up. First the neighborhood – it was nothing but boys and one other girl. You either learned to play ball, stand your ground and compete or you could live a very lonely existence in the house playing make-believe with dolls. Ick! With a big brother to keep me from real harm, I was confident, assertive and engaged. It fit my nature perfectly and probably disappointed my prim and proper mother on more than one occasion.

My true competitive nature can be laid directly at the feet of my loving grandmother, Essie Mae Wilson Holt. She was the youngest girl from a family of nine children. Her mother died young, shortly after delivering my grandmother's younger brother. Grandma was raised by her father and her older sisters. She and my grandpa had three children – a girl (my mom) and two boys. My mom was the oldest.

When my mother divorced, I was two. Mom went to work to support my brother and me. She worked a lot of hours away from us; therefore, I spent an extended amount of time along with my big brother, Larry, in the company of my grandmother. It was any child's dream. Grandma loved the outdoors and bestowed that love on both of us. We were her first grandchildren and she doted on us like nobody else. My mother called us spoiled and we agreed.

Grandma was a feisty little lady who was always in charge (a trait both my mother and I have acquired). She managed and administered EVERYTHING that went on in her home and on her land. Grandpa would listen, acquiesce, and do as she said. By the time I came along, Grandma had given up her work cleaning white ladies' houses. Grandpa worked at Santa Fe Railroads and was making enough, along with the produce from the land, to support the family. Grandma had plenty of time to spend with her two grandchildren.

The little acreage Grandma and Grandpa owned had everything a kid could possibly want – a creek to wade in, a swing set to soar to the clouds and a neighbor with horses to ride. In addition, there was always fresh produce from the trees, vines and patches planted on the land. Everything was fresh – strawberries, grapes, cherries, apples, black walnuts, pecans, corn on the cob, tomatoes, potatoes, greens, cabbage and more. We learned to pick fruits, eating more than we picked of the strawberries and grapes. We learned to recognize birds in the birdhouse Grandpa built in the tree next to the house. We learned that heaven was a salt shaker and a ripe tomato eaten on the back steps on a warm sunny Kansas day. We learned to appreciate the laughter and camaraderie of watching Grandpa and our great uncles playing horseshoes along the creek bank. They shooed us away so they could have grown-folks talk; but we always found our way back to hang out around the edges and watch the fun. They'd toss those shoes, talk a little trash and smoke cigars and pipes – all out of the reach of their wives who were back in the kitchen hosting their own grown-folks talks.

When we had to stay inside because the weather was rainy or too cold, my grandmother, brother and I played Chinese checkers. Grandma beat us unmercifully. She had no pity because my brother and I were young. It was then and there, I learned what true competition was all about. If you wanted to win, you had to be good enough to do so. With Grandma as my guide, I learned there were no excuses for losing. Winning is about preparing, learning, practicing, strategizing, and then executing --(like running a business.)

Eventually, I got better. I observed my grandmother and brother and their moves. I began to understand their tendencies and strategies. The first time I beat both, I thought I had conquered the world. And in some ways, I had. I knew I had finally won because I was good – not because they let me win. That is what competition is all about.

Of course, in playing Chinese checkers, everyone is playing by the same rules. It is hard to cheat, and you only gain the advantage by being better and craftier than the other players. In business, I learned that is not always the case. There are those who don't want fair competition. They are too afraid they are not as good as they think they are. Or they don't want to give up the power they have inherited because of their gender or heritage. They feel privileged and want to keep that privilege. Therefore, it is harder for minorities and women to compete. The rules are not geared to fair competition, but instead, to privileged competition. Why? Is it because the privileged are afraid it might turn out like sports? Those who have been held down might produce superior results? We might win and they might lose? Maybe they aren't as good as they think they are? (That's a discussion for another book.)

Thanks to Grandma, I don't use being a woman or a minority as an excuse to fail. I do use it to my advantage like any game I might play. I have studied the rules, examined how to use them to my advantage and tried to become the best I can be -- stand out (not hard to do if you are a woman and/or of color) in whatever I do. I have learned to play to win. *(Thank you, Grandma. Life is much the same as Chinese checkers – sometimes you win and sometimes you lose.)*

Doris Marie in her favorite independent color – RED!

FIERCELY INDEPENDENT

Noble and great. Courageous and determined. Faithful and fearless. That is who you are and who you have always been. And understanding it can change your life because this knowledge carries a confidence that cannot be duplicated any other way.

-- *Sheri L. Dew*

My own independent thinking I lay at the feet of my mother. I did not have all the obstacles placed in my way that my mother did. But, at an early age I knew I would go to college, get a good job and be "successful." It's the DNA she gave me, as well as the will to think I could do it.

There is nothing more inspiring than to have someone believe in you, and my mother was my biggest cheerleader. She reminded me that I came from a line of smart people, no matter where they finally ended up in life. Both my grandpa and one of my uncles were very good "with numbers." They worked for Santa Fe Railroad. Though they didn't have the chance to use their skills to the fullest, they were able to create a comfortable environment for their families. When my mother found out that I, too, was gifted with understanding and excelling in mathematics, she bragged about it often. How could a child not do well when their mother bragged to everyone that you were one of the smartest children around?

Her belief and push launched me into advanced mathematics classes from the fourth grade all the way through college. My mom did not know what you did with such knowledge, except become a teacher. However, in my junior year of college, I discovered the practical end of math – computer science. I fell in love with the problems, the solutions, the practicality of it all and earned a degree in computer science. I have been involved with technology and computers ever since.

I can recall a time when I was growing up that my mother showed her independence. My mom and dad had always bought any car she drove as a joint effort – going out reviewing the options with the dealer, determining the terms of payment and then driving away in the car. One winter while my dad was working in Oklahoma, my mom got fed up with her car not starting. She was raising us at home by herself and just got tired of waiting on dad to get home and get her a car that would run properly in the winter. She went to visit their favorite dealer. The next we knew, she came home with a Buick LaSabre. (Dad had always only bought Oldsmobiles.). It had push button gear shifts. When my dad did finally make it home for one of his long weekends, there in the driveway sat the Buick.

When my younger brothers were teenagers and in school all day, mom would take off from work and have her own fun getaway day. She didn't really drive on the highway. She only drove around town. But, one day she decided she was going to drive to Wichita, Kansas. It was a two-hour drive and I had lived in Wichita at one point. The highway or turnpike between Topeka and Wichita was a clean ride. Plus, the mall that she

Terri and her mom on a seven-day cruise that Terri gave to her mom as a retirement gift from secretarial work for the State of Kansas

and I visited when I lived there was right off the highway. She jumped in her car and drove to Wichita by herself for a day of shopping and relaxation. She returned home in the early evening with items from her shopping. By the time she did this, I was married and living in St. Louis MO. I heard about it from my dad and brothers who couldn't believe she just up and left them. I thought it was the funniest and most independent thing she had done in a long time for herself. All I told them was, "Go mom!"

But I gained something else from my mother and her genes – administration. She ran the office where she worked, even though she was only the clerk typist/secretary. The professionals depended upon her and she delivered. Anyone who could raise five children (four rowdy boys), work and keep a household had to know something about order and administration. Like many working women then and today know, multi-tasking and organization is a way of life.

I, too, found the bug to be able to administer. I often laughed with my business partner that we could administer anything. Give us the challenge and we can organize it, execute and make things happen! Sometimes you just must not think too long or hard about the situation and just do it! That philosophy has never failed me. While I have had some stumbles, like my mom, I just keep moving and it seems to all work out just fine.

Comfortable in My Own Skin

Not until I was grown and interacted more with other women leaders, business owners and executives did I realize that many were not raised to be confident and comfortable in their own skin. I attended conferences and participated in executive training sessions and was always amazed at the questions and conversations coming from these women. Sure, there were obstacles to succeeding. Of course, no one was just going to give you a chance without you fighting for it. What did they expect? Isn't that life? I attributed my confidence and comfort to being raised around four brothers and a neighborhood full of boys. You played sports and if you weren't good enough or felt sorry for yourself, you could spend a lonely existence inside playing with dolls! I think my mom would have liked me to play with the dolls and be a little bit more ladylike, but she never discouraged me from following around my big brother and participating with the neighborhood kids.

On the other hand, my mother encouraged all her children to read books. And, even as grownups, we all tend to still do that. I was considered quite the introvert at school growing up – an egghead, a smart kid, one who enjoyed the company of a book maybe even more than the company of people. Don't get me wrong, I enjoyed people when I was around them, but I never felt I needed them to complete me. My mom taught me that I had the skills and the brains to do anything I wanted to do in life, and I believed her. Those who know me now would probably agree that my optimism and belief in my own abilities (coupled with the great ability to enlist others to get things done) has served me well. While many today don't view me as an introvert, those who really get to see it know I can sit with a book and shut out the world. For a few hours each week or on the weekend, I do just that.

I guess because my mom was so extroverted and engaging, I never felt the need to talk much, just sit and enjoy and listen. Isn't that how you learn? Well, today I would tell you I learned well. Because, like her, I can engage anyone in a conversation and make them feel comfortable about talking to me. I can talk at their level whether they are a senior executive of some major corporation, a child looking for attention or a minority business owner trying to chart their dreams.

Thanks for the confidence, Mom and your amazing administrative skills!

The more a daughter knows the details of her mother's life [...] the stronger the daughter.

— Anita Diamant, The Red Tent

PART 7 - Spicy Southern Grits

A good cook is like a sorceress
who dispenses happiness.

--Elsa Schiaparelli

*T*he South gets a lot credit for something called Southern Hospitality -- warm, sweet, comforting and welcoming to visitors. (Of course, the discourse occurring while this book was being written has proven anything but hospitable. And others would even say the South has never been hospitable to those who weren't of a certain background or ethnicity. But that is a subject for another book.) What can be realized about the South is there are some people who are great cooks, have a welcoming disposition and enjoy entertaining others. Our **Southern G.R.I.T.S.** radiate hospitality and enjoy making others feel right at home. This is true whether you're eating some deliciously prepared food or business networking. In both cases, their mothers influenced their hospitable ways!

Giselle (GiGi) Fisher-Ray

CAJUN MAGIC...

Good cooks never lack friends.

--Unknown

Food is not far from any equation involving her. She's mixing, talking, directing and moving all the time. She's tall and lean. Hands with long thin fingers pound dough or gently add flowers to a centerpiece arrangement or reach to grab your hand in a moment of needed prayer. Her head is crowned in fashionable "au natural" twists that accent her large, tired, coal eyes and ready ample smile. Dressed in her business-branded polo, black jeans and comfy black rubber-soled shoes, she once reported at 3:00 am to a commercial kitchen for another day of food preparation for her business. Now, she has transformed her A Plus Events catering and event planning business into a more profitable, rewarding

191

and focused direction. She honed the business to one central and rewarding theme – The Gourmet Bread Pudding Company. The redirection has made all the difference in her work-life balance and has allowed her to enjoy her husband Kurtis Ray, children and grandkids at a much easier pace.

The Gourmet Bread Pudding Company is the most delicious bread pudding you will ever taste. The GBPC food truck can be found around the Dallas/Fort Worth area at festivals and shows, but if you get to know GiGi well, she might even cook up a batch for your own special party. Or, you might get invited to her home to enjoy watching the Cowboys or a boxing match. Then, you get to sample the real tastes of New Orleans.

New Orleans breaks through the surface as she talks, scurries, cooks, prays and laughs over food preparations. Giselle "GiGi" Fisher is a bona fide entrepreneur who injects delicious into every dish from tasty morning sausage burritos and cheddar cheese biscuits to spicy jambalaya for lunch or sauce-capped chicken served with her "secret recipe" tea or gourmet bread pudding at an evening event. GiGi touts the excellence, beauty, professionalism and caring ways of Southern hospitality. It springs from her love for cooking, planning and executing her dream. I tease her about her frou-frou business; but I've seen her when she turns a barren room into an elegant decked-out affair, working with a slim budget and compacted time frame.

I am not sure when I first met Giselle. I might have connected with her as she coordinated an event for a non-profit foundation helping to support breast cancer awareness among women of color. We have commiserated, celebrated and laughed over the experiences of being an entrepreneur. Sometimes it's good and sometimes it's challenging, but neither of us would have it any other way. This prayer warrior just keeps praying and moving forward.

Giselle's strong faith in God, penchant for catering and event planning and love of entertaining are a joy she inherited from her mother and grandparents. It is a mix of food, fun and family that make her the lady she is today. You've often heard the phrase "cooking with gas." Well, I think Giselle is fittingly "cookin' with grace." Here is where that all came from…

<u>Cookin' with Grace</u>

Delores Brown Fisher was born in New Orleans. She was the baby of the family with seven older siblings. She grew up in a family of love and faith. Her mom and dad owned a small catering company. They would get up early each day and cook food. Then they would take it around to construction sites and sell it to the workers. It was their early version of a food truck. Delores interned in the business and learned all about food

Delores Brown Fisher,
Giselle's mother

193

preparation, catering and decorating.

Delores married at nineteen. Her husband, Edward Fisher Jr., had been in the military. He worked at a retirement home and then as a postman where he eventually retired. Delores was an elevator driver for one of the prominent hotels in New Orleans before going to work in food service at the Veterans Administration (V.A.) Hospital. They had four children – three girls and a boy -- and were married for 50 years. Giselle was the middle daughter surrounded by sister Marie (nicknamed Bonnie), brother Marlon and younger sister Millicent (known as Millie).

Delores was a multi-tasker. She raised four children, managed a home, worked during the day and spent evenings and weekends involved in the church. She loved to cook and, on occasion, she catered parties. Delores and Edward were active participants in the local VFW chapter. Delores often traveled to different parts of the country for the VFW national convention each year.

Delores was a strong believer in God and her faith was the armor to deal with any circumstance. Her children were protected by her prayers and surrounded with the love of God and their family. If times were hard or times were good, Delores praised God and thanked Him for every situation and outcome. Delores also believed that faith was more than praying and going to church. She put her faith into action for others to see. She didn't need to preach; she just showed the goodness of God. She remained an active member of her church until her death. And if you wronged her or she was disappointed in you, you would never know. She would just erase you from her presence and keep on moving forward.

"Mom had the kindest heart of anyone I know," recalls Giselle. "If you were in need and she had it, she would give it to you. She provided Christmas gifts to the ministers at the church, the Sunday school teachers, her neighbors and friends. She just had a giving spirit."

Giselle also recalled how her mom loved to cook for others. They had a neighbor who played for the Green Bay Packers and traveled all the time. Her mom would cook meals and freeze them, so he and his family would have them handy.

Delores also loved the outdoors. In New Orleans, crabbing is a regional pastime. When crab season was at its height, you could find Delores crabbing down by the bayou. This outdoor-loving chef, however, was also a girly girl. She would wrap her head and stay far away from the mud. She didn't believe in getting messy!

Speaking of dressing, Delores loved to shop, dress elegantly (especially going to church or to a VFW function) and enjoyed well put together outfits. Clothes might not make the man – but they sure made this woman!

All About Cookin'

Food and entertaining naturally made its way into Giselle's blood. She grew up in New Orleans surrounded by her grandparents and parents. In addition to her mom and her maternal grandparents, her paternal grandfather loved to cook. He was a cook aboard a transport cargo ship. When he came back to New Orleans, he continued his cooking ways. He and Giselle's grandmother would cook for all the holidays. It was how Giselle got her start in cooking by handling the seasoning for the meals.

Originally, Giselle wanted to be a nurse. She never liked baby toys but loved to play with her brother's stuff. She went to Southern University and became interested in computers. She wanted to be able to make some money, so she earned a degree in technology. She was smart and navigated college just fine. Upon graduation she went to work for AT&T/Western Electric in Denver. She later moved to Dallas to work for EDS as a systems analyst. Giselle remained there for several years while she made a living and raised her son, Christopher. However, she knew all along that her true love was much like her mother's and grandparents'. She had always enjoyed cooking and she decided to take the plunge and put her love into action.

"I used to help with the family catering business," laughs Giselle. "I was young, but I was part of the wait staff. I learned the right way to do stuff and how to present yourself while waiting tables and handling food. It was a joy to be able to be a part of this experience and see so many people eating up the fabulous dishes my mom and grandparents prepared."

When Giselle made the natural move into event planning, she did so with the experience from her family.

Giselle began putting on events with a networking group formed with friends in Dallas. Her friend Lynette encouraged her to use her God-given gifts. She partnered with a company to increase her credibility, while she planned weddings, birthday parties and anniversaries. They bid on and won a catering opportunity for the National Minority Supplier Development Council Conference in Dallas. When the City of Dallas contract to provide food services at City Hall became available, they bid on the project and won. The partnership started strong and the partners worked well together.

But Giselle found herself limited by what she could do and how it should be done. When her partner decided to go back into the corporate world, Giselle transitioned into going it alone. She created A Plus Events and hasn't looked back. She found herself diversifying the event planning and catering business when she had the good fortune of winning a bid that put her into the kiosk business. Her "Grab 'N Go" business expanded into various locations around Dallas with several different companies. The experience took a lot of work and Giselle finally decided to concentrate in one direction and one direction only. She slowed her activities with A Plus Events, closed the kiosks that required her starting at the crack of dawn and, instead, concentrated all her efforts in The Gourmet Bread Pudding Company food truck business.

Mastering the coordination of personnel, recipes, locations and funding have put her faith to the test. But as

Delores taught her, "prayers must go up for blessings to come down."

When Times Get Tough – The Tough Keep Going

As is often mentioned throughout this book, times are not always rosy. It is often your attitude that determines your character and direction. Delores Brown Fisher was no different. She had arthritis at an early age and it progressed into multiple parts of her body as she grew older. For a chef and cook, that can cause distress and end the joy of cooking. It's a painful, crippling disease. Delores handled this the way she handled everything – with a strong dose of faith and a willingness of adventure. She didn't let the arthritis stop her. She went so far as to be an early adopter of knuckle replacement surgery. She was featured in an Arthritis Foundation magazine article about the surgery and how it worked for her.

As Delores aged, she continued to be on the go. She would go to bed earlier (sometimes six in the evening), but she was always up early and moving. She wouldn't let anything stop her from traveling to her VFW conventions all over the country, participating in the Golden Age organization, planning trips, coordinating activities and going to church. She maintained her volunteer endeavors with the Arthritis Foundation and the Golden Age.

When Giselle was pregnant and expecting in Denver, Delores flew to Denver to be with Giselle. She knew how hard it could be to raise a child but knew the challenges Giselle might face as a single mother, away from family and support, could be even greater. When Christopher was born, Delores was there for a month making sure the new family was okay before she returned to New Orleans.

"It was such a blessing," affirms Giselle. "She came in and took charge. She even reorganized my closet and kitchen so SHE could find everything!"

Delores continued to dish out mothering wisdom to Giselle. She knew the relationship was strained between Giselle and Christopher's father, but she encouraged Giselle never to say a disparaging word about Chris' father to Christopher. Delores just encouraged Giselle to do what a mother should do. And…she knew if her child and grandchild stayed in the church, the church would surround them with love and assist in keeping Chris on the right path. Giselle's father also played an integral part in developing Christopher.

Delores' sage wisdom proved to be correct. Chris graduated from college with a bachelor's and master's degree in just six years. He returned to the Dallas area, married and started his own family. No one could have been prouder of this accomplishment than Delores, Bonnie, Millie, Marlon, grandfather "Fish" and Giselle.

When Giselle decided to open her own business, there was no bigger cheerleader than her mom. She would call up

199

and ask how everything was going and Giselle would say all right. Delores could tell by the "all right" response that times were tough for the business. She would continue to encourage Giselle and tell her everything would be just fine.

Delores also left a strong legacy of family. Besides being the cheerleader for Giselle in raising her son and managing her business, Giselle also learned to listen and take advice from key people in her life. Her sister Millicent is one of her top advisors in business, as is son Christopher. If it doesn't pass the "M-C" (Millicent-Christopher) test, then it probably isn't a very wise business decision. They have been strong sounding boards for decisions related to taking on particular clients, businesses or diversification ideas.

Giselle is now married to a wonderful man, Kurtis Ray, who supports and constantly encourages her as a Godly woman and business entrepreneur. He can often be found helping out at events and perfecting the customer service experience. With a home, grandchildren and the chance to concentrate on The Gourmet Bread Pudding Company, Giselle has finally reached her stride and is moving into true peace and success.

Delores' legacy of cooking, faith and family have all helped position Giselle in a positive situation for growth and joy...as she continues to "cook with grace."

Patti Winstanley in one of her facilities

A REAL SOUTHERN BELLE

Generation after generation of women have pledged to raise their daughters differently, only to find that their daughters grow up and fervently pledge the same thing.

--Elizabeth Debold

Of all the ladies I know and interviewed for this book, Patti Winstanley can claim the title of "Southern Belle." She was born and raised in Mississippi. She spent all her formative years there and went to college in the deep South. However, you don't need to spend much time with her before you understand she may be from the South, but she has distinctly liberal Northern tendencies. In fact, she may be the least Southern Belle I know. She is a spirited and vocal lady about the things that really matter to her – women's rights and equality, children and education, networking and her businesses. Where that southern hospitality comes alive is in her practice of connecting people with other people. She does this nonstop and for no other reason except she is good at it and wants everyone to succeed.

Patti started her career out of college as a special education teacher. She always wanted to teach and had a place in her heart for special needs children. That should tell you plenty about her and her heart. Her degree was in special education and she quickly put it to work. But she also had the spirit of an entrepreneur. She took whatever project there was around school and turned it into a special event. (She did this as a child, too, and you will soon see where she got it!).

As fate would have it, Patti underwent a catharsis in 2004. Hurricane Ivan demolished the Florida Panhandle. At the time, Patti and her two brothers owned their parents' house on Navarre Beach in Florida. The home, in the small private and quiet community, had been used frequently when the siblings' children were growing up. But it was being rented as the children grew older, and the siblings and their families visited more infrequently. The hurricane demolished the beach house and the siblings lost everything. For Patti, it seemed like the right time to refresh and start anew.

One of Patti's sons had purchased t-shirts from Aztec Custom Screen Printing when he was in college and knew the owner quite well. Aztec Custom Screen Printing was founded by a student at the University of Austin who worked out of his dorm room. He and his wife grew the business and hit a point where they wanted to sell it. Her son helped put Patti in touch with the owner and in 2005, she bought all the assets of the company and changed the name to Aztec Promotional Group. Patti became the president of Aztec Promotional Group LP. Aztec specializes in screen printed and embroidered apparel.

Thus, her new journey began. She continued to buy equipment and companies, expanded warehousing space, improved operations and grew Aztec from its Austin base to Tucson and Waco. In addition, she added proprietary software and technologies to create a primary differentiator for the business. Aztec holds licensing agreements with several universities and entities and that helped solidify its base of over 3,000 customers nationwide.

The Southern Belle became quite the southern entrepreneur.

Meet Jane Ann Ellis

Jane Ann Ellis, Patti's mother, was born and raised in New Orleans. She came from a broken home and went from living in a big house in the big city to a small apartment. Her adult life would prove much different from her childhood. After marrying, Jane moved from the small apartment in a big city to a big house in a small city. There, she would find the place where she belonged, surrounded by friends, family and purpose.

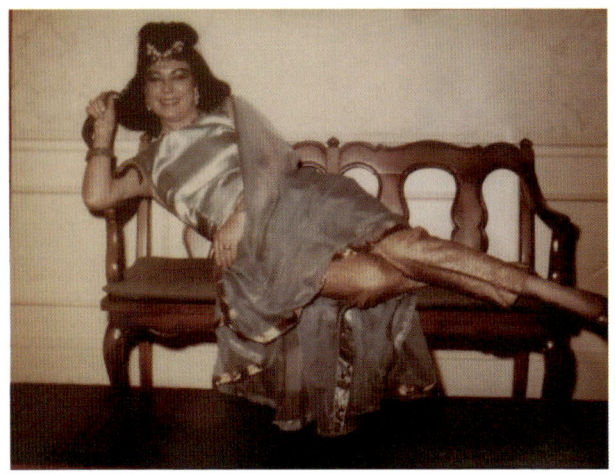

Patti's mother, Jane Ellis in her Cleopatra Outfit

She loved to entertain and was an incredible Cajun cook. She could whip up last minute dishes and the family always ate well. Mardi Gras was one of Jane's favorite times of the year. Her sister was a wonderful singer and worked in some of the nicest restaurants and hotels in the city. Jane always said, "I wish I could sing." The fact was she had a wonderful voice but never took the time to work on crafting it. There were more important things in life to her. Mardi Gras, however, was a different matter. The family would return each year to New Orleans for the celebration. Once Patti was in junior high, she was no longer allowed to go to Mardi Gras. Her mom didn't want her missing any school and would say, "never miss school because you night miss out on something important." Of course, what Jane was really saying to her daughter was that education was important.

Jane loved throwing her own parties, but also enjoyed attending parties. Every year, the local country club threw a costume party to benefit charity. Though it was not Jane's party, she acted like it was. She dressed up as Cleopatra, laid about on the couch and had her friends fan her!

Jane and her friends never worked outside the home. Patti said, "Growing up in a small town in Mississippi was a different life. Life was slow and jobs for women were very limited. Plus, I didn't grow up seeing many opportunities for women."

Instead, Jane was involved in school, PTA, civic organizations and the garden club. After all, it was important to have good schools for their children, a better community and green parks and flowers to present the right environment. This probably could be viewed as the quintessential way of life in the South. Patti recalls one year, her mom let the high school club make thousands of homemade rolls in the kitchen to sell for a fundraiser. Flour was everywhere for weeks afterward, but the team raised money to support their efforts!

Wear Clean Underwear

You didn't really think we would write a book and not include the most famous momism of all time – "wear clean underwear because you never know when you'll be in a wreck." (Does that imply something about women drivers or what?)

Anyway, it seems more than appropriate that a version of this momism should be used in the context of looking at our Southern Belle. Patti says, "I never thought my mother could give me outstanding business advice because she never worked outside the home. I used to roll my eyes and get embarrassed when she gave this advice in front of all my friends as I headed out the door."

What Patti discovered was that this might have been the best advice she ever received from her mother. It was Jane's way of telling Patti to always be prepared. Even when Patti was a young working mom with twin babies of her own (two sons), and she felt stressed out dealing with a project she didn't have ready, her mom would yell out, "Always wear good underwear, you never know when you will have a wreck!" Patti has tried to follow the "be prepared" advice and has even passed it along to her kids.

Despite any challenges, Patti has taken on her mother's spirit of fun, people and projects. She loves meeting and working with people. One of her companies is staffed by women between 25 and 82 years old, mostly retirees who have been sewing their entire adult lives. They bring a world of knowledge and continue to provide handcrafted artisanship that has been passed down for generations. And with Patti, you are never a stranger for long. She will walk you around the room and make sure you have the chance to meet others, especially ones with whom you can do business with. You enter her circle and you become the current project for improvement!

Jane was quite the character and she left a strong legacy for her daughter to follow.

PART 8 - Hominy Grits

A mother's love for her child is like nothing else in the world. It knows no law, no pity. It dares all things and crushes down remorselessly all that stands in its path.

--*Agatha Christie*

*P*eople who serve others with their life's work are special. **Cheese and Grits** is one of those grits dishes that make us feel good, comfortable and cheerful even if we are not a true grits fan. Every mother and daughter in this book have a faith geared toward giving back to others less fortunate. But the women featured have learned it from their mothers and have taken it to a whole new level. Faith, service and belief in a cause bigger than what you can see drives these women. The realize it is not all about us. Shirley Chisholm once said, "Service is the rent that you pay for room on this earth." I'd say these women and the mothers who raised them should be living in penthouses!

Lorena Valencia and her mother, Celia Valencia

RIGHT IS RIGHT--THERE IS NO GRAY

The most comfortable pillow in the world is that of a clean conscience.
– attributed to Celia Valencia

You hear her long before you see her enter the room. She sounds like a rapid-fire auctioneer explaining the priceless vase up for sale. She's not loud, just fast talking.... hardly taking a breath between her words. She's excited and excitable! When she comes into sight, you spy a woman barely five feet tall and maybe 90 pounds soaking wet. Her raven hair and big eyes are surrounded by hands flying as she talks. You are in the presence of Lorena Valencia -- CEO (or She-E-O, as she likes to say) of multiple companies. She is a whirlwind of movement and activity. You might guess she's a New Yorker or from the Jersey Shore – in your face, unabashed, aggressive. But in fact, she's a Hispanic from Chicago who now lives in Arizona. And yes, she does talk fast, and she acknowledges it. Don't get her excited about something – how can you tell?

Lorena Valencia is one of the smartest people in the room. Like others in this book, she's an entrepreneur. She founded a company in a male dominated industry – Reliance Wire & Cable and built it into a world-class company primarily servicing the automotive industry. The firm manufactures wire and tubing, primarily supplying clients like Toyota, Honda, Ford, GM, Chrysler, Tesla and Mercedes. In early 2016, she sold the company and decided to "retire."

Lorena found retirement a bit boring. She had always dabbled in projects and companies tied to technology while running Reliance Wire & Cable. When I met her, she was buying up various website domain names and reselling them to the highest bidder. This was long before most people knew the value of a domain name and GoDaddy was still a fairly new entity. By November 2016, Lorena had decided to completely pivot away from manufacturing and launch a new technology company, Fitz Media Corporation.

Not one to rest on her laurels and always driven by the next challenge, Lorena is taking on the proverbial Titans of the Internet with her latest investment and offering. If you've heard of Yelp, TripAdvisor, AngiesList, Twitter and Instagram and blockchain, then you will like her two platforms -- BravoCoin.com and ReBuzz.io. Users can earn cryptocurrency for posting comments, curating content and writing and rating reviews of restaurants, hotels, services, doctors and much more.

I met Lorena in her role as the chair representing minority-owned businesses in Arizona. She became part of the national leadership and we immediately hit it off. She had great questions and ideas about how to connect minority businesses, so they could do business with each other. She also shared her contacts and I did the same with her. Even today, we see each other at the various conferences about women and minority business and make sure to make the time to talk and compare notes. She enjoys the company of people and that fits right in with my way of life as well.

Absolute Integrity

"My mom always taught me to value honesty above all other things," says Lorena. "When I was about eleven, she said something that has become a tenet I live by. 'The most comfortable pillow in the world is that of a clean conscience.' To this day, I live by that motto of honesty and integrity. I mean what I say and say what I mean. So, I live without any regrets about how I comport myself or treat others."

For Lorena, the greatest lesson is to live by the truth. Another one of her mom's sayings is "you can't block the sun with a finger..." meaning the truth will always come through. In the business world, it is sometimes hard to always live by the truth. It can mean a deal or no deal in certain circumstances. But for Lorena, she says, "I walk into any room with my head held high, no fear and no regrets for things that I have done or said."

Lorena laughs when she tells the story of her mom not even believing in "white lies." A lie is a lie – white, black or gray, according to Celia Valencia.

Celia Valencia immigrated to the United States because it was known as "the land of opportunity." She was raised on a ranch in Mexico and went to school for just one year – the first grade. Yet, despite not knowing how to read in any language, she was fearless enough to come to the U.S. for a better life. She left behind her family, her friends, her belongings, her history and everyone she knew – never to return.

It's no wonder she truly believes there is nothing her children cannot accomplish. She learned how to read in her thirties by reading the Bible. Through courage and faith, Celia has raised three children – Lorena and her two brothers. Celia was a home engineer who dedicated her life to her children. "She was the chief inspiration, disciplinarian, nurse, chef, chauffeur, counselor, hair dresser, alarm clock, teacher and referee," laughs Lorena. "She still lives for our happiness. If I can be half the mom that she has been, my children will surely thrive."

Balanced Self-Esteem

Celia taught Lorena to be humble but never to feel that

Celia Valencia

she was better than anyone else or that anyone else was better than she was. It's a balanced self-esteem that has served Lorena well in meeting, relating and negotiating with executives throughout the business world. Celia's strong commitment to faith allows her never to have a sleepless night. "Her faith is so real, it is palpable," says Lorena. "In fact, some Bible verses still give my mom chills. She lives in full truth at every moment…"

Faith has made Lorena fearless, confident and a serial entrepreneur. It is no wonder she had no trouble dealing in a "man's world" in the automotive industry. She understands such interactions provide her something valuable to share with others. Balanced self-esteem allows her to feel comfortable, confident and secure around all people regardless of their "status."

Lorena tells the story of her speaking at an event during International Women's Day. When asked by the participants how she deals with challenges, she responded "I love it when someone tells me NO. It puts me in sixth gear." What she said next not only was a hit but resonated with the audience. "I look challenge in the eye and give it a wink!" You'd have to know this short, petite dynamo to really appreciate that she welcomes the chance to prove her stuff and is fearless in the face of doubting naysayers.

Now married with a young son, Lorena just bubbles when she talks about her family life. I ran into her recently at a conference and she was making sure she walked the floor of the expo, mingled with the right people and then headed back home to Phoenix to be with her family. It's great to be a successful entrepreneur, but it is even better to have someone to share it with.

The Philanthropist

When asked what her childhood ambitions were, Lorena responded, "I wanted to be a philanthropist. I was 10 years old when I decided that is what I wanted to be." It's no wonder that Lorena feels this way, with the faith imparted by Celia, the love of people, the respect of those less fortunate and a giving, faithful heart. One of the foundational tenets imparted to her by her mom and that she lives by is "those who give, gather."

Lorena started a non-profit called the FRDM Foundation. The foundation is leveraging e-learning, solar and a microlending business model to bring education to remote areas of the world. "Education is the absolute key to empowerment and personal freedom" says Lorena.

And, while Lorena describes her mom as an optimist almost to a fault, it is clear the apple has not fallen far from the tree!

Joyce Robinson

GOOD BOOK. GOOD LESSONS.

I have no greater joy than this, to hear of my children walking in the truth.

--3 John 1:4

I met Joyce Robinson at church, of course. I had moved to Dallas and was working in a telecommunications partnership business where I was a general partner. I had not taken the time to meet other people outside the industry but decided one day to do so. One of the easiest ways to meet people tends to be to go to church, but which church? While I was searching for a church home, I ran across a small local newspaper that highlighted a church that seemed to be a lot like my church back in Kansas. I decided to visit. One of the first people I met was Joyce Robinson. She made me feel right at home and soon I found myself not only going to church service but being a part of Mission One. Now, Mission One was for the more senior ladies, but they were so friendly and took me under their wing, that I chose to stay with them instead of the group closer to my age. Joyce was the chair of the Mission and that also made it more amendable to me. I later found out that her husband, Walter, owned the small newspaper where I found about the church. God does move in mysterious ways!

Joyce's story and that of the influence of her mother punctuates the power of faith and obedience to a higher power.

There Is Always an Answer to Any Situation

Contributed by Joyce Ann Robinson

My family was very involved in the church, and I got a firm sense of ethics from my mother, Nancy Ann. From an early age, my mother instilled in us the importance of consulting the Bible regarding all situations in our life.

When I was in high school, I recalled having a conversation with a friend on the phone. My mother was close by and overheard everything that was said. My friend was sharing how she had overheard another friend's boyfriend calling me a free loader. Even though I had often gotten rides from them, I had also given them rides as well. The thought that they felt I was taking advantage of them was very upsetting to me. I could not wait until my friend came over to my house, so that I could go into detail about what had been said.

I knew this information was totally erroneous. Besides, at the time, I was dating my future husband Walter, and this couple had ridden with us a number of times. Plus, my father always made sure any time I was out that I had spending money. He knew how cruel young people could be. He never wanted me to be dependent on anybody.

By the time I got off the phone, I was about to explode. I couldn't wait to let my thoughts be known about this issue. However, before I could say anything, my mother pulled me aside.

She reminded me what the Bible stated in Matthew 18: 15-17:

> *"Moreover, if thy brother shall trespass against thee, go and tell him his fault between thee and him alone: if he shall hear thee, thou hast gained thy brother.*
>
> *But if he will not hear thee, then take with thee one or two more, that in the mouth of two or three witnesses every word may be established."*

My mother let me know in no uncertain terms that I could not gossip about this situation. She even went one step further by telling me until I got over being angry, I couldn't even address the situation with my friend's boyfriend.

At first, I was disappointed because I couldn't believe that everything that we did had to be based on what God thought about the situation. Then my mother shared something with me that helped me get an insight to her position on consulting God about all major things in her life.

Joyce Robinson and her mother, Ann Hite Anderson

When my mom was a teenager, she had played the piano for the church. One Sunday afternoon there was a dance, and she decided to go to the dance instead of playing for the church. She caught the boat across the bridge to where the dance was being held. On the way back, the boat caught on fire. She prayed to God just to be able to return home safely. When she got home, she made a commitment that whatever was to be done for God would come first.

Even though it was difficult for me to embrace my mother's philosophy, I realized that her way did work. Over the years, I began to saturate myself with the word of God. As I got older, I found myself looking at a situation and consulting God before I moved forward. Throughout the years, I have been involved with several women ministries. I have made it a point to make sure that women don't tell me things that are going on with other women. I always remind those who are around me that they have a higher calling. There is always a still small voice in my spirit saying, "What would God do?"

My mother's lesson is now a very valuable part of my life. I seek God about everything that I do. I know that His wisdom will speak volumes into whatever is going on in my life – no matter how big, or small it is.

Gayle Waldron

THE GOLDEN RULE

Even as wisdom comes from the mouths of babes, so does it often come from the mouths of old people.
– *Mohandas Gandhi*

Wherever there's laughter and chatter, you are sure to find Gayle Waldron in the midst. She is a walking force of energy, vibrancy and fun. A ready smile mirrors that of her mom's.

I met Gayle while attending an executive management program produced by the Amos Tuck School of Business at Dartmouth. We were both in a program for women business owners designed to take our businesses to the next level. Amidst all the learning, fellowship and fun, we discovered Gayle had turned to a systematic method to find her next husband. Before the success of E Harmony and other online match-making sites, Gayle developed a list of criteria the next man in her life would have to meet. She was distributing the list to her friends and family for referrals.

This tactic is not surprising to anyone who knows Gayle. She is an organizational development consultant and just put her efforts to use to benefit her personally. Gayle is the founder and president of The Management Edge, an organizational development consulting firm. Gayle talks about the firm as a "not-for-profit only" business. She says, "…It is about making a living in an ethical way that genuinely improves the work situation for clients, therefore contributes to the client, the larger 'community' and the company."

These are not just words, or a snazzy tagline used to differentiate her company. It's one of the lessons she learned from her mother and syncs with her strong belief system based upon "The Golden Rule."

The Golden Rule

Gayle and her mom, Evelyn Ford Waldron, on a cruise celebrating her mom's 90th birthday

Gayle is the oldest of four daughters and one son. She says, "Do unto others as you would have them do unto you. This is a very big life lesson that my four siblings and I credit our parents, especially our mother, with teaching us. It guides us every day, in every decision. My mother was one of the most empathic people I've ever known. She truly believed that before you act, you need to put yourself in the other person's position."

Evelyn Ford Waldron lived a full life focused on family, helping others, laughter, love and dancing! She was known for her amazing needlework and sewing but best loved for her sense of humor and love of experiencing different cultures.

Gayle recalls, "Related to the empathy issue is my mother's unshakable belief in the essential value of each individual and that we each deserve respect. She basically related to everyone the same way -- with openness, interest, sharing, and an assumption that they have a great deal in common with each other."

Evelyn traveled the world and made friends with people in all walks of life, everywhere she went. At one point in her life she regularly traveled to Pakistan, Indonesia and Egypt, where Gayle's sister lived and worked. She loved adventure and traveled to 13 countries. She rode a yak in the Himalayas, a camel on the beach of Karachi, Pakistan and sunbathed in Bali! She was always enthusiastically welcomed at every spot she visited.

World travel also produced insight into cultural traditions and differences around the world. That peephole led her to question why people could hurt others or damage their self-esteem. It was one of the things that made her temperature rise and anger flash across her face.

Gayle's company was built upon harmonious living. The Management Edge is dedicated to change management, team development, cultural understanding and conflict resolution. The company guides leaders and employees through systematic methods to effect peaceful changes. Her innovative work in organizational development with the Department of Defense, Department of Energy and the U.S. Environmental Protection Agency saved the federal government millions of dollars. She is a recognized speaker in the States and abroad on issues related to the workplace, personality assessment, conflict resolution and women in leadership. She has won numerous awards for herself and her company.

Like her mother, Gayle gets angry over injustice and biases in the workplace and the community. She is an active leader and participant in several organizations making a difference for women, minority and small owned businesses across the country. She is a national founding partner and member of the board of directors for Women Impacting Public Policy (WIPP). This organization has been instrumental in advocating on behalf of women-owned businesses doing business with the federal government. WIPP efforts have produced significant changes in the past couple of years in certifying women-owned businesses and how they do business with federal agencies. The aim is to reach the minimum target level of five percent purchasing goals set for women-owned businesses. Advocating for rule changes and enforcement is part of the fight Gayle views as necessary to help level the playing field.

Fun Is an Important Part of Life

While equity and justice are serious topics Gayle has addressed throughout her career, there is a fun and funny side to her as well. You can always find the funny side of things if you choose to look. According to Evelyn, "seeing our own foibles is exceedingly funny." "My mom was a great story teller," chuckles Gayle. "Many of her funniest stories are about her life. She grew up in a very poor family, yet her childhood was invariably filled with humor. Her humor was legendary and drew people to her."

It's no wonder that when Evelyn turned 90, the idea of a cruise excited everyone she knew. She celebrated her 90th birthday on a cruise to Mexico with family and friends (over 80 people). At 95, she celebrated with a dance party. "Mom was a very blessed and popular lady!" Gayle laughs.

Gayle, too, has a host of friends and family. She has two wonderful sons who live with their families about 1800 miles from her. Her first two grandbabies, both girls, were born three weeks apart in the month of March. She now has five granddaughters and one grandson. They occupy much of her thoughts and heart. When she began to look at the lessons her mother taught her, Gayle just wanted to be the kind of grandmother her Mom has been.

I suspect Gayle has plenty of stories to pass along to her grandchildren about her life, their fathers and their grandmother.

<u>Volunteering Your Gifts</u>

Gifts and talents are designed to be shared, Evelyn believed. Helping others is always worth it to you and to them. Evelyn always volunteered to do things for others and enjoyed life more because of it. She would sew, cook, drive people places and even cleaned houses and nursed the sick, when needed.

Gayle declares, "One of the reasons helping out came so natural to my mom is an awareness of how blessed and how lucky she had been. She knew how easy it was to be a victim of circumstance and how much a personal connection and willingness to lend a hand could mean."

Gayle clearly garnered several lessons from Evelyn that has served her and her company well!

Author's Grandmother, Essie Mae Wilson Holt

FAITH BASED

To find your place in the sun, you have to leave the shade of the oak tree.

--African Proverb

I have had the pleasure of speaking to young people, wannabe entrepreneurs and business people on my journey and the life of a corporate-rogue-gone-entrepreneur. While I can and do talk about business, planning, marketing, strategic alliances and finances, one aspect I most enjoy discussing is that leap of faith as an entrepreneur. All these ladies in this book, whether running their own business or someone else's, at one time took a chance on themselves. And that has made all the difference in their journey.

In one speech I made to young women students at my alma mater (Kansas State University – Go Wildcats!), I was still working in Corporate America. I was the top female African-American in the company at the time and many wanted to know how you do it – achieve in Corporate America. My two patented answers have been and continue to be: 1) Confidence that the Creator who made you made you uniquely to achieve, and 2) Faith that that same Creator is always there for you. These two premises can see you through good and tough times and instill a confidence not dependent upon what others think.

I can't remember when I didn't go to church. My mom and grandparents made sure my brother and I had a strong foundation in faith. My grandpa was a deacon and my grandmother a deaconess. Sunday meant we got up and went to Sunday School. From there we all went out to grandma and grandpa's for dinner before heading home later in the day. Often, aunts, uncles and cousins were there enjoying delicious meals with fresh vegetables and lots and lots of conversation! It was somewhat like the movie "Soul Food" with the kids at the "kiddie table" and the grownups at the big table in the kitchen. Throughout it all was an understanding at church that you went to learn, be quiet and be respectful. At home, you could laugh, enjoy and be a little bit rowdy.

I was 12 when I accepted Jesus Christ as my Savior and was baptized into my family's faith. That faith has seen me through many a situation – especially as a business owner. I often laugh and tell people, "If you want to test your faith, become an entrepreneur!" Because no matter how great the business plan, financing, talented people and marketplace, there will come a time when you wonder, "Why did I do this?"

In fact, there is no way I would have created a business plan that has directed my life the way it has. (That, too, might be a topic for another book.) Clearly, my Creator has had something in store for me each step of the journey. And even when I haven't always listened, I have always looked to my faith in my Creator and what was created in me to sustain and guide me.

As Zig Ziglar says, "You are the only person on earth who can use your ability." Or as some youngsters say, "Only you can do you!"

Faith brings you through and my mom and family taught me that early on.

In search of my mother's garden, I found my own. -- Alice Walker

PART 9 - Stone Ground Grits

I believe in love at first sight.
Because I've been loving my mother
since I opened my eyes.
--Unknown

*L*ike many women in this book, the next set of ladies were clearly impacted by their mothers. **Stone Ground Grits** are made from grain that is slowly ground by a traditional stone mill, so the grits retain all their natural oils (the heart of the corn). They are cooked smooth and creamy and retain the full rich natural flavor of the grain. No better allegory could be used to describe these women than **Stone Ground Grits** who have honed their skills and dispositions into delivering excellent service to their clients and the communities in which they live.

Carrie Brewer Martinez and her mom, Judy Brewer

IF PICTURES ARE WORTH 1000 WORDS...

When the first baby laughed for the first time, the laugh broke into a thousand pieces, and they all went skipping about.

--Peter Pan from Finding Neverland

Perhaps the first thing you notice when you're around Carrie Brewer Martinez is not her, but her magnificent work. If you are fortunate enough to be invited to an event where her work is on display, you are so engrossed in what she has done that you may overlook the short, pixy cute blond who is behind the piece. Don't fret over it. Her work is that good, and she will make sure you know who she is before the event is over. She is an observer of life and characters, a

233

consummate storyteller and a lover of people! Carrie is a clone of her mom. They are alike in some of their ways, as well.

Responsible Caretaker

Judy, in Chesapeake, Virginia with Carrie at age 21 months

Judy Brewer was born in Dallas, Texas. She grew up about a mile from where Carrie now calls home. Judy was the second oldest of two boys and four girls. The house was filled with the six children plus her maternal grandparents. She went to Catholic schools and was always very responsible and giving. As the oldest girl, she took on the role of responsible caretaker. Today, she continues much the same role as manager, bookkeeper, and advisor for the family office of a prominent family. She is a problem-solver and this role fits her persona. Judy went away to the University of Texas after graduating from high school. The financial burden on her family caused her to return home after just one year. She moved in with her sister, found a job and went to work. It was the responsible thing to do. The sisters happened to live near a young man, Ben, who would soon become Judy's husband. Six months after meeting, the couple married. Judy's new husband longed to be an aviator and immediately entered the Navy and officer's training in Pensacola, Florida.

For a young woman who had not been far from home, the move to Pensacola, followed by being stationed in Virginia, was a challenging proposition. It was a long way from the comforts of Dallas and the reinforcement of her family. Her husband was at sea a lot and she found herself pregnant with their first child – Carrie. Eventually a son, Curtis would also follow (he was born in Corpus Christi, Texas). While her husband was at sea, Judy raised and cared for their two children miles away from family and friends.

"I can't imagine how difficult it was for my mom," states Carrie. "My dad was at sea for months at a time as a Navy pilot. He traveled during my entire childhood and my mom raised both me and my brother, often with no help from family since we lived so far away."

To add to the difficulties, Judy's mom developed cancer and passed away. Carrie was just two or three at the time. Curtis had not yet been born. Judy was just in her 20's raising a daughter by herself and mourning the loss of her mother while light-years from home. She shouldered on. She had been a caretaker of others much of her young life – with younger siblings and now with her own child. She knew what to do and she just did it.

When Ben retired, the family moved back to the Dallas area. Carrie was ten by then. Her dad took a job as a corporate pilot. That kept him on the road as much as when he was in the Navy. By then, however, Judy was near her father and siblings.

Quiet Leader

Sometimes it is not what you say, but what you do that makes the difference in where you want to go. Carrie learned this simple fact from watching her mother be a persistent, problem-solving, quiet leader. It is a lesson that has served Carrie well on her road to a successful business.

"My mom used to tell me 'if you can't say something nice to someone, then don't say anything at all," recalls Carrie. "I must have been a very bossy, critical little girl because my mom told me this a lot."

Following Judy's example of moving forward no matter what, Carrie learned to temper her enthusiasm and "rightness" in a positive direction. The producer on a film is often the underpaid project/product manager. They oversee EVERYTHING, making sure it happens as planned. They are the problem solvers when things don't go per plan. They must make sure all of it happens within the timeframe and budget allocated for the project. It is often their vision, money, and time on the line if it doesn't.

"I manage some clients who maybe aren't the most creative," understates Carrie. "But of course, they think they are. In the creative world, there are always egos and emotions to manage. In the back of my mind, I hear my mom saying, 'be nice and don't be bossy.' I guess the fact that I have learned to temper my comments with wisdom and constructive feedback results in what I need my clients to see."

Carrie has learned to manage work relationships and tell her stories. She has learned the art of problem solving passed down by her mom. She started her career in broadcast journalism and worked in television news and consulting. She traveled the world, producing in-flight entertainment for United Airlines. After a while, she realized she had learned all she could from the company and at 29 decided to parlay her skills into a company of her own. She wanted the latitude of telling a more controlled story at a higher production level. CM Productions, Inc. was born.

Balancing Motherhood

In all of Carrie's travel and hectic work schedule, she never forgets the importance of her family. Her husband, two sons and parents are all central pieces in her life.

Judy puts family above all else. In raising her children, many times alone in a distant place, she wanted to make sure her children knew they were a gift that she took very seriously. Judy has worked much of her adult life. Yet, she always made sure her children came first. She loved and encouraged her children, while reminding them to be kind and considerate of others. She staunchly supports Carrie's career choices and backs her actions all the way. She never told Carrie not to do something. Instead, she encouraged her freedom of choice and backed her decisions whether she agreed with them or not.

Judy also believes in seeking the joy in life. "She loves to put on parties," shares Carrie. "She is very creative when it comes to decorating, hosting parties and crafting special gifts. She likes to make little things and remembers everyone's birthdays – including her nieces and nephews."

Carrie's two sons have felt this love and joy. Each Monday, "Dooda" as the grandchildren call her, spends time taking care of her grandsons. There is probably no more enjoyable time in the house than when "Dooda" arrives for duty. It allows Carrie to spend quality time on her career, and it allows Judy to spend time with her grandchildren— important to both.

"I know one thing," affirms Carrie. "My mom has made me appreciate the importance and role of being a mother. Watching her with my sons is so pleasing. It makes me so happy to see her laughing and playing with them. And it makes me value being a mother even more myself. As a mother myself, I truly appreciate her more every day."

Royalyn Reid

LEARNING TO HAVE AN IMPACT

Mama exhorted her children at every opportunity to 'jump at the sun.' We might not land on the sun, but at least we would get off the ground.
--Zora Neale Hurston

The first thing you might say after meeting Royalyn Reid is that she is striking. She's the girl next-door with a ready smile, friendly personality and refined demeanor. And, once you get to know her, you realize it is all for real. A corporate person turned entrepreneur, she has studied the art of entrepreneurship and executed from the lessons learned. While the winds of the marketplace may shift from time to time, she remains rooted in improving, pivoting and building her business. Planning and execution are foremost in her vocabulary. This is not surprising since her training has been centered around education, market research and delivering impact. She gets paid to find out what you think – whether it is deplaning at the airport, determining the global marketplace or evaluating consumer products.

Royalyn is the owner and co-founder of Consumer & Market Insights (theCMIteam). "We believe that insight without action is incomplete," says Royalyn. "The purpose of learning is the first step in effecting change in processes, sales, service, culture, communication and more."

CMI is a marketing research and training company that adds a unique approach by taking into consideration human experience factors based upon emotion and behavior. provides market research, training, event planning and more. While Big Data and Artificial Intelligence can assemble lots of data and analyze what has happened, CMI includes the human factor to help predict where to go next. CMI has offices in Dallas/Fort Worth and Washington DC and supports clients the private and public sector throughout the nation and globally.

This assimilation of educational facts into practical solutions came easy to Royalyn. After all, she comes from a lineage of educators. Her mother, Billye Batiste Rayes is a retired professor of Health and Kinesiology at Texas Southern University (TSU).

<u>Living to Be Impactful</u>

Billye Batiste Rayes is the friendliest and most engaging person you might ever want to meet. It is not hard to see why her students, family and friends are enthralled with her. Whenever she is in the room, you feel right at home, and Billye has no problem engaging you in a conversation on any subject.

Billye Batiste Rayes

Billye was born in Jacksonville, Texas, a small town a few miles south of Tyler, Texas. The family was very active in education, politics and business. Billye's mother was a school teacher who later became a school principal and entrepreneur. The family started and owned one of the funeral homes in town. Billye's sister was the National Secretary for Top Teens in America, an organization dedicated to providing teens extra-curricular support, career and character development and community volunteer opportunities.

The family was focused on education as the key factor for success. Billye was good in school and loved sports. She was a starting point guard on the basketball team. She was exceptional at her sport. In fact, her father thought the team did not appreciate Billye's talents enough. The story goes that she was encouraged to show up late for the game -- letting the team play without her for a bit. They found out how important she was. They were losing the game when she arrived and entered the game, All were relieved – students, parents and players – to see her.

From her high school days, Billye went on to play basketball at Texas Southern University. She majored in Kinesiology and put as much effort in her studies as she did her court play.

"I never once had to interview or seek a job," says Billye "I went from the classroom to graduate assistant to professor at TSU."

Billye believed in the power of education to change people's lives. She knew how it had changed her life and she paid it forward every chance she got. She taught health, but also taught life to the students that came through her class. She worked with the statewide committee on education, planned parenthood and was extremely active in working with her chosen political party.

While she was teaching at Texas Southern University, she had the pleasure of meeting an athletic coach. That encounter would change the trajectory of her community and educational involvement, as well as that of her daughter. She was a single mom looking after her own mother when she met the man who would help her deliver more impact than she could imagine within the community.

Coach Larry Joe Rayes, an assistant coach at TSU, and Billye would eventually marry. Athletics and coaching seem to fit easily into Billye's world of kinesiology, which engulfed physical therapy, health, rehabilitation and sports and exercise. Coach Larry Joe left his job at TSU to eventually become the head of the athletic department for the Houston Independent School District. He developed award-winning innovative teaching methods to enhance his students' understanding of math. The move provided Billye the opportunity to develop and implement her own game plan for academic achievement. She assisted students in making a seamless transition from high school to college. She worked hard to help them understand the potential and opportunities that lay ahead by attending college. Plus, she encouraged, guided and supported them in understanding the rewarding and fruitful impact higher education could have on their lives.

The couple coordinated many events and awards for Houston athletes, including TSU track. In all their activities, Billye made sure to always be available and engaged in her daughter's school activities. She enjoyed gathering a group of kids and taking them to new places to experience the world outside their everyday world. She wanted them to imagine bigger and better things beyond their existing circumstances. Along the way, she encouraged Royalyn to be active in sports and school activities – making the journey impactful and fulfilling.

Billye also understood and loved football. She joined her husband in his activities, as well. Perhaps it was always meeting and talking with new people that excited her or just the love of seeing students succeed in whatever they tried. The family believed in the power of sports, positive school participation and continuous education to change lives. The couple built a legacy of learning and impact that helped change the trajectory of many young diverse students in the community.

Houston Bred. North Texas Led.

Royalyn was born and raised in Houston, Texas. She attended public schools and was active as a cheerleader and drill team member. She also played volleyball and was one of the star players. A coach tried hard to recruit her to play in high school, but the lure of her friends and cheerleading won out.

Upon graduation from high school, she attended the University of North Texas in Denton, Texas, where she studied psychology. She had always been fascinated by the subject of psychology and people. She followed up by obtaining her master's degree in human development from the University of Texas in Dallas. She didn't stray far from the pathway established by her mother. But she took it a step further. Upon graduation, she began her corporate career as a R&D scientist for Mary Kay. There she delved into consumer insights and consumer product testing. She worked at Mary Kay for 10 years.

After their first child was born (a clone of the family genes she named Madisen), Royalyn and husband Angelo decided now might be a good time to step out on her own. It would give her more time with her child and she had learned a lot from her experiences at Mary Kay. She entered the world of consulting. She worked with Hattie Hill, a well-known consultant specializing in marketing, international management consulting and leadership development. Her own consulting practice began to grow, and Consumer & Market Insights was born. Her first real contract was with the DFW International Airport. Her entrepreneur direction took off.

Royalyn did what her mother had taught her to do. She dove into the entrepreneurship experience, networking, attending functions, getting additional training and talking to any and everybody who could impart knowledge related to growing her business. She signed up for courses over time with Harvard School of Business, Tuck School of Business at Dartmouth, Wells Fargo Executive Education Program and more. She believed in continual learning, planning and executing on her plan and that directive continues to drive her and her business.

In one of her networking sessions, she was introduced to a person with HUD in Washington, D.C.. There was an opportunity to do planning for HUD training sessions around the country. The sessions produced a nationwide opportunity and expanded the company into further contacts, federal government and other planning opportunities. It also introduced her to the advantages of becoming an 8(a) contractor and additional opportunities with the Department of Transportation Smithsonian Institution and Department of Commerce.

Help Is on The Way

As CMI took off, Royalyn found herself doing what most mothers and working women do – juggling career, business, home, husband and children. By then son Royce Parker had been added to the family. Billye and Coach had

Three Generations -- Billye Batista Rayes, Royalyn Reid and daughter Madisen Reid

retired and decided to move to the Dallas area to be closer to their daughter, son-in-law and grandchildren. They could help with the children and enjoy the relaxed life of retirement. However, after a few moments of retirement in their Carrollton, Texas home, they decided it would be more fun to work with Royalyn and the CMI team. After all, they were masters at conversation and networking. At one point they traveled with Royalyn and her team putting on more than 25 events around the country. They were listed on the team organizational chart as business developers, but they were CMI's superstars. Wherever they went word had already arrived about this engaging couple

246

working at CMI. Billye was the hit. She talked, laughed and encouraged everyone as if they were her child. She continued to encourage and support her daughter and the CMI dream. At the writing of this book, Billye is still active with Royalyn and CMI and continues to be the superstar on the team.

Royalyn participated in the PEACE THROUGH BUSINESS® training and mentorship program for women entrepreneurs in Afghanistan and Rwanda. As part of the experience, Royalyn, her husband Angelo and Billye traveled to Rwanda to encourage and assist women entrepreneurs in Rwanda grow their businesses.

Billye's Mission Statement

You have probably heard of creating a personal brand, but have you ever stopped to think what your mission statement is. Billye has. Here is hers:

Lord, help me to make a positive difference in the lives of others.

Billye gets up every morning and repeats her mission aloud to herself. Wow! What a power and lesson to be learned by all. No wonder she has been so impactful in the lives of the youngsters she has met along the way!

For Royalyn, Billye has taught her to have a vision, a mission, a plan and to execute. Foremost, she has encouraged Royalyn to pay it forward.

Wanda Granier

EXCEPTIONAL CUSTOMER SERVICE

My mother is my root, my foundation. She planted the seed that I base my life on, and that is the belief that the ability to achieve starts in your mind.

—*Michael Jordan*

Wanda Granier is the energetic, enthusiastic, radiant CEO and majority owner of BridgeWork Partners, a fast growing, award-winning talent acquisition firm specializing in information technology, human resources consulting and administrative services staffing. She is also a proud graduate of the University of Texas (with the logo attached to her photo on the company website!)

It's not always timing that determines success. Sometimes it is just about the right formula, people and ability to execute that determine the road to achievement. Wanda opened BridgeWork Partners with her business partner, Amy Legate, in 2008 during the Great Recession. But their emphasis on "take care of the customer or someone else will" has led to a very successful business in a highly competitive field. Later, a third business partner was added – Samantha Jacoby. Samantha, a millennial, was the firms first full-time hire and proved herself so valuable that Wanda and Amy made her a partner. Also, the move was a testament to the company's commitment to supporting women.

How did Wanda get so savvy about business? She attributes the entrepreneurial spirit to her dad, but her mom taught her what extraordinary customer service is all about. As business owners the world over will tell you, there is no business without satisfied customers.

<u>Smart and Caring</u>

Mary Matta Dutchover was born in Presidio, Texas, a small rural U.S. border town located at the junction of the Rio Grande and Rio Conchos. Mary was raised and went to school in Pecos, Texas, but became quite sick with tuberculosis when she was young and had to drop out of middle school. She was never able to finish her formal education.

She met and married a young man named David Dutchover, Jr. and they made their home in Pecos, Texas. Pecos is one of several small west Texas towns founded and

Mary Matta Dutchover

organized around a train depot. It is known for hosting the first ever rodeo in 1883.

Mary married David and they had six children. Wanda was the fourth. Mary was primarily a homemaker and volunteer. But her quick mind and friendly personality proved useful as an administrative assistant to her husband at the Reeves County Teacher Credit Union. David was the president of the credit union, as well as the Assistant Superintendent of the Pecos Independent School District. Mary cared a lot about people, and you could see it in her actions and her eyes. When she worked at the credit union, she made every person feel like she had all the time in the world to handle their concerns and issues. She listened earnestly to each individual and treated them with kindness and compassion.

"My mother was always there for us," boasted Wanda. "She said the right encouraging words and had the ability to brighten the day, lift spirits and express her love and support. She had a very high emotional intelligence and it showed in everything she did and said."

Mary's caring ways extended to her own parents, brothers and sisters. She was always there when they needed a helping hand, and she enjoyed having the entire extended family over for meals at her house. She was an excellent cook and very Christian lady. She enjoyed helping others in the community and staying involved with her family. She was a constant volunteer at the school and local Catholic churches. She took food to the sick, visited the elderly and shut-ins and helped throughout the community. She was the first one to offer a helping hand if someone was sick or suffering.

From President to CEO

"When I was a child, I told my parents I wanted to be President of the United States," said Wanda. "While I didn't achieve that, I think I have had the opportunity to provide real leadership and impact in my business and within the community."

Wanda began her talent acquisition career working at Veritude, an internal staffing resource for Fidelity

Investments, one of the world's leading providers of mutual funds and financial services. Veritude meets the temporary staffing needs of Fidelity managers by recruiting candidates in information technology, finance and accounting, business marketing, office administration and customer support. The positions held at Veritude served Wanda well in understanding and learning about the business of talent acquisition.

When she decided to chart her own path with the development of BridgeWork Partners, she now had the skills and ability to build teams, win clients and develop long-term partnerships and a client base. Her three main principles in running her company can be attributed to the lessons learned from her mother: 1) take care of the customer, 2) make a difference in the community and 3) build a team culture committed to individual and team growth.

"My mom made everyone she encountered feel special," said Wanda. "I think that lesson has had the most impact upon me when dealing with my clients. Extraordinary customer service is having the ability to make sure everyone feels special, heard and understood. We try and do that every day at BridgeWork Partners, and I think it is the singular reason for our success and growth."

Mary's Lesson on Giving Back

Mary's commitment to the community was not lost on Wanda. In all that her team accomplishes, they are a very active segment of the community in which they live.

"The heartbeat and foundation of our company is built on our 'BridgeWorkGives' program," states Wanda. "We operate with a strong passion and spirit to provide positive impact in the communities in which we live. We are strongly committed to community outreach and allow each of our team members to volunteer up to 10 hours per quarter during work hours."

Wanda practices what she preaches. She has been involved in numerous volunteer activities for cancer research benefitting M.D. Anderson in Houston, Texas, American Cancer Society Relay for Life and Jonathan's Stage, benefitting Leukemia and Lymphoma Society. She proudly participates in the 77-year old Greater Dallas Hispanic Chamber of Commerce, where she previously served as Chairman of the Board of Directors. In addition, she has served on several business and chamber boards in the community. She has been recognized for her work in the community with several awards, and BridgeWork Partners has been acknowledged as Supplier of the Year regionally and nationally. The company was named #2 Best Place to Work in Dallas three times and once was listed as the #1 Best Place to Work!

"My mom lit up the room with her spirit and enthusiasm for life," declared Wanda. "That enthusiasm has definitely rubbed off on me. But, perhaps the most important thing she taught me was to forgive people, have faith in God and live my life walking in the right direction."

We would say Wanda has learned these lessons well. She makes work fun, expects the best from her team and ensures each person she meets feels at home in her presence.

PART 10 - Chocolate Sweet Corn Grits & Berries

With a child's heart
face the worries of today...
-- *Henry Cosby, Sylvia Moy, Vicki Basemor*

If you're like me, you don't think of grits as a dessert dish. Sure, you can add some fruit to them and call it dessert. Imagine cookies and pies made with grits or **Chocolate Sweet Corn Grits and Berries.** *In other words, grits can be fun and so can you. Mothers taught their daughters several heavy lessons, but they also encouraged them to live life and have fun. Celebrate the moments. Take time to take care of yourself. Relax. You are better for everyone when you're in good shape and spirits.*

Gail Warrior Suchy

JUST DANCE...

When you find yourself on thin ice...
you might as well dance!
-- Unknown

Pumpin', droppin', poppin' to the pulsating beat is where you can always find Gail Warrior at a party. She is the one in the center of the dance floor, beaming and stepping. A tall, slim drink of rich chocolate in six-inch stilettos and a short, slim fitting dress made to accentuate the positive, Gail Warrior believes in playing (or maybe we should say partying) as hard as she works. Whether it's taking on the challenge of "how low can you go" as she effortlessly bends to touch the floor or negotiating a contract with a government official, the one thing you recognize quickly with Gail, is that she is a dynamic force of nature.

Gail Warrior founded and captained the largest woman-owned modular construction company in the country. She started the company from scratch and built it into a leading corporation by the time she was 40. So, it's no wonder after dealing all day in a world dominated by men, that when it was time to play, she was just as commanding, in charge and passionate. An avid hiker and body builder, Gail is adamant about taking care of her body and mind. One of her favorite stress relievers has always been dancing. She loves to dance. Not necessarily artistic dance or choreographed modern dance or even ballet or tap (though, I am certain she could easily master any of these). No, Gail just likes to party!

Behind that veneer is an intelligent, strong, leading business woman who has built several successful businesses. The Warrior Group proved her acumen acquiring the right talent to take a business to the next level. She strategically charted the course of Warrior Group and succeeded in a male-dominated environment.

I met Gail as a part of the Dallas/Fort Worth Minority Supplier Development Council. We both owned businesses and shared a respect and love for the President of the organization, Margo J. Posey. I watched Gail and her businesses grow and thrive due to her unfailing focus, unparalleled skills and passion for life. That intensity for work, fun and "paying forward" are all part of the lessons she learned from her mom.

About Dancing…

Dorothy Jean Mitchell Warrior

For those who knew her mother – Dorothy Jean Mitchell Warrior – Gail's love of dancing is no surprise. When times get tough, when times are easy, when times are simply times…you can always dance! Dot, as most of her friends affectionately called her, always enjoyed music and the dance floor.

Dorothy was born in Mt. Pleasant, Texas. She was the oldest of two children and attended elementary school in Terrell, Texas. She later moved to Dallas, Texas and graduated from Booker T. Washington High School and attended Bishop College. Dorothy met and married Melvin Warrior and had three children – two girls and a boy. Gail is the middle sibling.

Dot worked in Corporate Human Resources at Texas Instruments during the 1970s and '80s. The conservative corporation had great people who had a sense of community and commitment. Dorothy Jean Mitchell Warrior fit right in. By day, you could find her in her role as an Executive Administrator around the TI campus working, talking and enjoying her colleagues. Everyone loved her at TI. It didn't matter your race, gender, creed, etc. She would talk to everyone and even though she told you what she thought, she was very empathetic at the same time. On more than one occasion, employees who wanted to file EEOC claims with the company, found Dot's sage wisdom helpful and decided not to file lawsuits.

On the weekends, it was time to kick back and enjoy more of life. With house parties often held at the Warrior home, Gail had a front-row view of the excitement and fun.

"My mom was so beautiful inside and out. She loved to dance. She loved to cook!" chuckles Gail. "I learned my famous butter pound cake recipe from her, and she learned it from my grandmother. Mom loved to give of herself to others, especially me, my siblings and my dad. She was, in short, my superstar, rock star, would-do-anything-for-you mom. Now make no mistake, she wasn't perfect, but with all of her imperfections she was the perfect mom for me."

"My mom had a passion for dancing...even without a partner," says Gail. "She would be up in the middle of the floor dancing alone if she had to. There was never a party without delicious home-cooked food, pulsating music and endless dancing. It was one of the things I remember most about my mother. It is probably why I am so passionate about dancing. My mom's zest for life exemplified who she was. She never found a party she didn't enjoy, or a dance floor left lonely. She could dance until the last beat of the music and keep right on. She taught me so many lessons, but this one sticks with me day to day."

Dot, Gail and that philosopher, James Brown, all agree...

"The one thing that can solve most of our problems is dancing"

Hey Mister, D.J., put the music on...

Never Stop Learning

Like most of the women included in this book, Gail heard over and over from Dot to get a good education. But Dot also encouraged her children to never stop learning. There was always something new to experience and learn. She, right along with her children, believed in doing just that. Dot worked around engineers and thinkers every day and saw the difference a good education could make in life. She saw great thinkers at Texas Instruments, whose inquisitive minds constantly asked the question "why not," created some of the most important inventions in our lives today. Dot wanted her children to have all the opportunities the world offered.

Gail attended and graduated from Clark University in Atlanta with a degree in accounting. She received her corporate training from Mobil Oil, followed by a master's degree in marketing from the University of Dallas.

She continued to learn and grow as CEO of Warrior Group. She took her namesake seriously and was a warrior in business. It is why she could envision a modular construction company owned by a woman, when she started on a shoestring with the help of family and friends. Warrior Group excelled in a field totally dominated by men selling to the military and government. Warrior Group took a mentee position with one of the nation's largest construction companies in order to learn more about handling larger opportunities, as well as construction management. After 18 years of running the company, Gail retired from Warrior Group and decided to move on to other endeavors.

Her experiences leading a large diverse company were worthy of note. She turned the experience into numerous speaking engagements helping women and young people understand the dynamics of successful living and entrepreneurship. At the same time, she turned her workout passion into a business called Warrior Elements, a luxury active lifestyle brand that empowers individuals to cultivate the Warrior within. She designed, manufactured and sold the workout brand around the world.

Eventually in her travels, she met a young man who had an amazing business that was impacting the healthcare industry and making the world a safer place in which to live. Christophe Suchy has helped revolutionize safety overseas.

Gail, never one to pass up a great opportunity, not only married Christophe but the couple formed a new company on October 31st (Halloween) and ironically called it the CASPR Group. Gail serves at the new company's CEO. CASPR Group is focused on reducing pathogens found in the environment, especially in health and food markets, that may lead to illness. One product developed by CASPR has shown success in reducing bacterial, viral, fungal (mold) and volatile organic compounds (e.g. benzene, ethylene, formaldehyde) levels by up to 99.9% for surface and airborne applications. The couple is focused on growing the U.S. market for CASPR products and creating healthier environments for people worldwide – something that fits right in with Gail's commitment to a healthier lifestyle and Dot's lesson on continual learning.

To Whom Much Is Given….

To whom much is given, much is expected. Dot believed because God blesses you with exceedingly great gifts, it is your responsibility to not hoard them but to share them. Dot lived her beliefs. After 36 years at TI, she did not just stop, retire and sit down. She continued giving back in her community by volunteering at her church and the Senior Center in the Hamilton Park community of North Dallas.

Gail carried on the support of the Hamilton Park community while combining the love of learning with cultural experiences. Out of her involvement grew the Heart of a Warrior Foundation. Its mission focused on "…generating, executing and facilitating programs and resources that provide total enrichment opportunities that are educational, cultural, experiential and life enhancing through programs targeting underserved children." The Foundation provided tutoring and educational support and growth and introduced the children to the amazing culture within their own communities. Begun in 2007 with 50 children, the program has grew to over 400 children serving the Dallas area. It was created to give young children experiences they wouldn't necessarily receive otherwise and ensure they are on the right educational track to make a difference in our world.

Combining education and cultural experiences, Gail has broadened Dot's lesson to a wide community and the families within it.

Today, Gail travels the world working with the CASPR Group and helping to impact the lives of children and adults to make a better and healthier world for all. Dot would be proud of the impact her daughter has had and continues to have on the lives of people worldwide.

*Author's mother opening Christmas gift
of a mother's ring*

HOLIDAYS THAT BIND

The most important thing she learned over the years was that there was no way to be the perfect mother and a million ways to be a great one.

-- *Jill Churchill*

In my mom's world, holidays and birthdays were major affairs. After all, she would remind us, she was there for each of our birthdays! It wasn't about the presents. It really was about the cake. It was the laughter, the teasing and the gathering that made the occasion special. As we grew older, it was a card in the mail with $2.00 enclosed and a phone call

265

to let us know how important we were to her. My brothers and I still laugh about the $2.00. Maybe it could buy a McDonalds Value Menu item! We knew no matter how far apart we were physically, we were loved and thought of on our day of birth. She made sure we celebrated each other's birthdays, our Dad's birthday and anyone else in our extended family.

Of course, the joy and happiness extended to her birthday, too! She expected her birthday to be just as special. Not one of us would or could forget March 22nd – her birthday. We found ourselves buying special gifts, calling to say, "we love you," trying to make it home when we could.

Christmas was even more festive. The season officially began when Mom put up the tree the Friday after Thanksgiving. Out went the nuts, cookies, a large candy cane under the tree for decoration only; no one could touch or eat it. There was usually a sprinkling of presents, no matter how strapped for cash she was. She even had a train on a track that encircled the tree. Imagine! What a "Wonderful Life." We thought everyone lived like this!

My favorite Christmas memory involved a gift I gave my mom. I was a young college student, tutoring math and English on campus to make ends meet. I had made a little money and I decided to put a "mother's ring" on credit to give her for Christmas. It was my first credit purchase and the local college town jeweler extended credit knowing I would pay for it. Looking back, it wasn't much – probably ten carats. She loved it, nonetheless, and wore it for many years because it came from me.

I also remember when I was grown, married and working for Southwestern Bell Telephone Company. I lived in St. Louis at the time. I had earned a lot of miles on a luxury airline carrier that traveled between Kansas City and St. Louis. They had first-class seats throughout the plane and top-level service, as well. Mom had never been on a plane; she loved trains. I cashed in my miles one summer for her to fly to St. Louis to spend time with us. My brothers and Dad drove over in the car. She loved the plane ride and thought all planes were luxury like this airline. I think she was a little disappointed in subsequent trips to visit me in Texas when she flew coach class. (I would hate to imagine what she'd think about flying today!)

My mom sacrificed so much to make holidays special for us. Even today, as grownups, we all are still little kids when it comes to the holidays. My older brother disparaged his friends who didn't see fit to wrap their gifts to him. Unwrapping a gift was as important a part of the celebration as the celebration itself. There were no gift cards or gift bags. She expected and we followed suit with well-thought out gifts that were properly wrapped and delivered with a smile. It didn't matter how much you spent, just that you thought about it and could show a little love.

Mother made our lives exciting in every way she could, and that love has bound our family even tighter through the years.

Author with brothers, dad and mom during a Christmas gathering.

As my brothers grew up and had kids of their own, Mom wrapped her arms around each of her grandkids with the same love (and even more it seemed). It didn't matter if her sons had made questionable choices for mates. The resulting children were part of her. She had a rainbow collection of grandchildren – black, part Japanese, part white, part Native American, part Hispanic…but they were all her kids, all her family. We were multicultural before the word existed. My mom could probably teach a few people about the power of diversity and acceptance. She claimed each of her grandchildren unconditionally, just like she claimed anyone who came into her house with one of us. I marvel sometimes at how big her heart was and how blind she seemed to be to the outward person. She loved people and she "cursed" each of us to love them, too.

Epilogue

A mother's love is the food of life.
--Unknown

For those of you who like to turn to the back of the book and read the ending to see if the overall book is worth reading, I commend you for your time-saving dedication and hope you take the time to enjoy the stories of some very remarkable ladies.

One thing that is not specifically said throughout the book but is the top condition passed along from these mothers to their daughters is LOVE. Everything these mothers did in terms of example, sacrifice, encouragement, listening and more was couched in love. No matter what religion or belief you may have about your Creator, it is clear to me that the greatest force in the world is love.

A new command I give you: Love one another.
As I have loved you, so you must love one
another.

By this everyone will know that you are my
disciples, if you love one another. John 13: 34-35

With that as the backdrop, here is a summary of key lessons delivered from mother to daughter:

- **Faith** in something bigger than you is essential for both the good and bad times. Have faith that you're not alone and it will all work out the way it was intended. Faith also includes forgiving, treating others right and being respectful of the differences. Our Creator made us all and made no mistakes.

- **Confidence** in one's abilities can make a world of difference into what you become. Believe in yourself despite the naysayers because only you can be you. This might be the best gift a child can receive from a parent.

- **No Excuses** opens the door to think bigger and do more. Do Y-O-U! Concentrate on your strengths, not your weaknesses. You can do more and go further by doing so. Don't let labels, stereotypes and the opinions of others define you. Always consider the source – are they even someone you respect?

- **Circumstances Do Not Define Your Trajectory.** Time after time, women have overcome their circumstances to achieve greater good. These mothers and daughters are proof of that. It is true for you, too!

- **Family Is Important.** Whether it is your blood family, adopted family or a supportive network of friends, support of others in you can make life so much more fun and purposeful.
- **Forget Lean In – Stand Up!** Leaning makes you susceptible to falling over and being walked on. Plant your feet and stand up for what you believe – your dreams, your values, your direction. Assimilation is not always the answer. Ask The Artist. Where others tread might not be meant for you.
- **Continually Learn.** Always be encouraged to reach out and learn more about your profession, the world, other cultures, other people. After all, you don't have ALL the answers. Collaboration can be an exciting thing and learning can take you to new heights.
- **Give Back.** Paying forward is not just a good thing, it is the only thing. Because in the end, it is not all about you. Look what these mothers did for their daughters and communities. Imagine what this world would be like if it were led by women like these mothers and daughters.
- **Never Give Up.** No matter what your dream, your Creator placed you in a spot to learn and grow. Never give up on being all that you can be and using your Creator-given talents to make a better world for yourself and others.

- **Don't Forget to Have Fun.** Life is short. While you're overextending yourself to handle situations with others, don't forget to stop and enjoy the moment. Someone needs you in their life, so make sure to treat your body, mind and spirit to the very best you can. Be healthy.

Whether we confirm or deny it, our mothers have a tremendous impact upon who we are. In the case of the woman entrepreneurs or business executives in my life, many have been positively influenced by their moms. Some may feel, like a few associates of mine, that their mother's impact doesn't define who they are today. They felt their drive was influenced by others like a father or teacher or grandmother. I am sure that is true. There are always more factors than one that make us who we are. But, for a few of these ladies and what I know about their mothers, I would say they are wrong. There are some quite glaring similarities. That, however, may make it into another book!

Finally, I have worked around this book for several years. In December 2018 a close friend, advisor, warrior told me to just go get it done. She gave me a journal and a pen for Christmas and said, "Go be a writer. That is what you are!"

I took her advice. I booked my first solo trip to a secluded resort in Ambergris Caye (San Pedro) in Belize and started to finish what I started. I organized, wrote and rewrote stories, all while enjoying sunshine, pools/beaches, great food and solitude at the Sapphire Beach Resort. The natives kept asking, "Are you traveling by yourself?" I would respond, "Yes. I'm a writer and I came for the quiet and sun to finish my book." I would get the same response around the Tiki Bar in the evenings as I sat on a bar stool nibbling on delicious ceviche and drinking wine with fellow travelers. Couples from Virginia, Austin, Texas and Kansas City became my regular cohorts around the bar each evening. They would tell stories of the best places for snorkeling, excursions to try and beaches that were better than where we were staying. I, on the other hand, spent my days enjoying intense poolside writing, relaxed walks along the beach, 83-degree temperatures and magnificent views of the water and boats. It was exactly what I needed. No phone calls (although I texted and sent photos to a friend each day to say I was okay and writing). No emails or business to take care of. Just an all-focused effort to complete this book. I did take a day

The author in Belize

excursion to see the Mayan Ruins. Wow! I even climbed to the top of one 112 feet up in the air. It just proves there were plenty of smart people in the world before we arrived and there will be plenty after we are gone.

I know there are lots of stories out there because everywhere I have gone and mentioned what I am working on, someone wants to tell me their story. Several of the ladies around the Tiki Bar loved the idea of the book and wanted to make sure to get copies when it was released. For all the stories that did not make it into this book and that you want to share with others, please reach out and submit your thoughts at **www.givemeGRITS.com**. We are hosting an experience for women worldwide to share their stories and the lessons they have learned from their mothers. We would love to hear from you.

Love you always, Doris Marie and Thank You!

Terri Lee

A Few More Quotes

A daughter is one of the most beautiful gifts this world has to give. – Laurel Atherton

~~~

God bless the child who's got his own.
-- Billie Holiday

~~~

No matter where you're from, your dreams are valid.– Lupita Nyong'o

~~~

All that I am, or hope to be, I owe to my angel mother. --Abraham Lincoln

~~~

Mother is the name for God in the lips and hearts of little children.
--William Makepeace Thackeray

~~~

I got to grow up with a mother who taught me to believe in me. --Antonio Villaraigosa

~~~

I am sure that if the mothers of various nations could meet, there would be no more wars. – E. M. Forster

About the Cover

The Artist at work plus her mosaic found in Terminal D at the DFW International Airport.

The painting found on the cover of **Give Me Grits – Girls Raised Intentionally To Succeed** was provided by award-winning artist, Viola Delgado. A part of her unique story and the impact of her mother are included in this book. She is an imaginative artist, painter, and sculptor who is driven by an incredible passion for self-expression through art. Her works are often noted for their unique simplicity, vivid color and elegant geometrics. Viola has developed an innovative style that blends precise realism with abstract expressionism. We asked Viola about her artistry and the painting on the cover.

What is the painting called?

Viola -- I call it Mami Arriving or Mommy's Arrival (mami llegando in Spanish). A tall, slender and well-dressed lady with a valise heads toward a house. In the window, watching the arrival is a young girl and older woman. There are lots of assumptions you can associate with the painting, however, part of how I paint is to allow the viewers to build their own relationships and meaning into the painting.

What were you thinking about when you painted this piece?

Viola -- This particular painting relates to a story about my own grandmother. When she was very young, her mother (my great grandmother) left the family and never returned. No one ever knew or said why she left. There was plenty of speculation. She was a beautiful, tall, slender woman and just one day, she just up and left. I can remember growing up and sometimes catching my grandmother just standing with her hands on her hips looking out the window, as if she was looking for something or someone to come to the house. I imagined she was looking for her mom to return. Her bed always faced the window and the bed in the painting symbolizes my own grandmother's room. The long skirts, shawl and braided hair also reminds me of her and her upbringing. Unfortunately for her, her mother never returned. My painting, in a way, is in tribute to her and her longing.

The young girl in the painting is the first time I did a painting with a child. She is wearing a blue dress. On my 10th birthday, I had a dress much like one in the painting and it was one of my favorite dresses.

We noticed that you have done several paintings of women but never paint their faces. Why?

Viola: Yes, this painting is from a series of paintings I have done called Las Manitas, or translated, it is slang for little sister. I think of the series as being about sisterhood.

I don't paint the faces because it allows the viewer to relate more to the painting. They can imagine or be reminded of someone they know. The long skirts, braids and color are part of my Mexican heritage, but also tell the story of women who are respectful, solid, strong and unbroken. These women, much like my mother, created strong families built upon faith and love. No matter what their circumstances or obstacles in life, they always looked ahead toward the future for both themselves and their families.

People always wonder how artists get their ideas.

Viola -- My brain is like a ticker-tape banner constantly flooded with images, even in my dreams. Some of these visuals demand to be on canvas more than others. For me, art is an everyday, 24-hour experience that I live, eat and breathe. The lines, concepts, texture and color just come alive for me. I never sketch a piece. I just paint what I see directly onto the canvas.

I know it's a gift, but it can sometimes be distracting when I am trying to concentrate on curating a show or working with a corporate or public sector agency on artwork for a project. But it is who I am, and I enjoy sharing my gift and works with others. It has started many great conversations and built wonderful relationships.

(Note from the author...I can attest to Viola's 24/7 attention to art. If you have lunch with her and a napkin is handy, she's always doodling. Or, if a child is with us, she encourages the child to doodle right along with her!)

About the Artist

Consciously adopt the mindset of a young child, to whom all of life is a grand adventure. Life is your playground.
--Jonathan Lockwood Hale

Viola Delgado has exhibited in several solo and group shows throughout Texas and the nation. Her career started as a social worker for the Dallas Independent School District. But in 1986, she left stability behind and struck out on her own as an artist.

Her art career includes teaching art to young people, curating art works at various art centers in the Dallas/Fort Worth area, including the Latino Cultural Center in Dallas, Texas and organizing amazing exhibitions of Latina arts. She has created huge public and private murals, a 20-foot glass floor mosaic located at Terminal D in the DFW International Airport and was the first ethnic artist to create an entire exhibit at the Dallas Area Rapid Transit rail station.

Viola attended the Art League School in Alexandria, VA and Dallas Baptist University in Dallas, Texas with a major in psychology. She was born in Sinton, Texas and resides in Dallas, Texas.

To view additional Viola Delgado artwork and/or purchase original pieces, visit http://violadelgado.com.

Of all the haunting moments of motherhood, few ranks with hearing your own words come out of your daughter's mouth.

--Victoria Secunda

About the Author

On the darkest days, when I feel inadequate, unloved and unworthy, I remember whose daughter I am and I straighten my crown.
--Unknown

Terri L. Quinton is CEO and President of Q2 Marketing Group LLC, an award-winning, full-service marketing firm primarily focused on the business development and growth of small and mid-sized companies. Her firm works to assist with messaging and in connecting to prime target markets in the most economically and efficient method. A serial entrepreneur, Terri is also co-founder and Managing Principal of the Alliance of Diversity Printers LLC (ADP-LLC), a printing, warehousing and fulfillment firm with a national footprint that is strategically aligned with printers around the country.

Terri began her career in management positions at Southwestern Bell Telephone. Her fast-track career included stints in the data center, the comptroller's staff, product management and new product/service marketing and sales.

She left SWBT as the highest ranking African-American manager out of 70,000 employees to pursue a partnership in an entrepreneurial telecommunications company.

Throughout her career, Terri has always been an avid writer and reader. She credits her successful career to her ability to readily understand complex concepts, convert them into everyday English and present them to a target audience.

"I love to write. It is what completes me," says Terri. "Several years ago, I started a book to honor my mother. She was a strong influence on who I am. I started writing and interviewing my friends but had a hard time figuring out why anyone else might want to read something I wrote.

The original title for this book was **Mothers and the Lessons They Taught Us.** *But with all the books about mothers, I couldn't quite get a grip on the direction. I just wasn't sure what these women and their mothers were trying to tell me. Finally, I realized people are always looking for principles that have helped us live our lives. And these women had such amazing stories of strength, courage and hope to tell. Plus, my friend Margo J. Posey, charged me to just go do it! It was the push I needed to move forward."*

Terri is more than an entrepreneur and writer. She is committed to efforts to help women of color and young entrepreneurs grow their businesses and gives willingly of her talent and time to organizations empowering minority and women entrepreneurs.

> *"I would like our school systems and organizations associated with young people to encourage them to create jobs, not just get one," said Terri. "Innovation often comes from striking out on your own and not being afraid to fail. Perhaps the most exciting thing to me right now is that a niece and nephew who have been around me, are working on building their own businesses. I am delighted that the entrepreneurial spirit is rubbing off!"*

Terri is a member of the board of directors for the National Minority Supplier Development Council (NMSDC). Terri was the first female elected to chair the NMSDC Minority Business Enterprises Input Committee (MBEIC), representing over 17,000 minority owned businesses and 1,000,000 employees nationwide. She served in this position for six years and represented minority-owned businesses as the sole voice on the senior-level Executive Committee NMSDC. She is part of the executive committee board of directors of the Dallas/Fort Worth Minority Supplier Diversity Council and a board member of the Women's Business Council – Southwest. She volunteers with WINGS (YWCA) to assist young women entrepreneurs in the area of marketing their businesses. Terri is active in several initiatives dedicated to encouraging more women and minorities to enter fields related to science, technology, engineering and mathematics (STEM).

She has been recognized with numerous awards for her work and commitment to diversity and inclusion. She was inducted into the Women's Business Enterprise Hall of Fame in 2016 for her business acumen and dedication to women entrepreneurs.

Terri holds a Bachelor of Science degree in computer science from Kansas State University and an MBA from Southern Illinois University- Edwardsville. She is a graduate of the executive business management programs at Kellogg School of Business at Northwestern University and Tuck School of Business at Dartmouth.

Terri is an avid sports fan, mystery and historical fiction reader, red wine lover and traveler.

She is originally from Topeka, Kansas but makes her home in Dallas, Texas surrounded by a variety of friends, business associates, a niece and grand nieces and nephews.